SURVIVAL ENGLISH

English Through Conversations

Book 1 - Teacher's Manual

SECOND EDITION

Lee Mosteller

Bobbi Paul
San Diego Community Colleges

Illustrated by Jesse Gonzales

REGENTS / PRENTICE HALL, Upper Saddle River, NJ 07458

Acquisitions editor: *Nancy Leonhardt*
Electronic production/interior design: *Paula D. Williams*
Cover design: *Marianne Frasco*
Pre-press buyer/scheduler: *Ray Keating*
Manufacturing buyer: *Lori Bulwin*

Printed in the United States of America

20 19 18 17 16 15 14 13 12

ISBN 0-13-016643-X

Prentice-Hall International (UK) Limited,London
Prentice-Hall of Australia Pty. Limited, Sydney
Prentice-Hall Canada Inc., Toronto
Prentice-Hall Hispanoamericana, S.A., Mexico
Prentice-Hall of India Private Limited, New Delhi
Prentice-Hall of Japan, Inc., Tokyo
Pearson Education Asia Pte. Ltd., Singapore
Editora Prentice-Hall do Brasil, Ltda., Rio de Janeiro

Contents

Preface   vii

Introduction   1

Coping Skills Chart   2

Scope and Sequence Chart   4

Teaching the Visuals   6

Teaching the Dialogues   7

Literacy Practice with the Work Sheets   9

Charts   9

Reading Passages   11

Activities and Games   13

Teaching the Picture Page   14

Total Physical Reponse   14

Using the Supplementary Work Sheets   15

SURVIVAL ENGLISH (page by page)   17

    Unit 1 – *Personal ID*   18

    Unit 2 – *General*   26

    Unit 3 – *Family*   35

    Unit 4 – *Health*   40

    Unit 5 – *Transportation*   46

    Unit 6 – *Food*   52

    Unit 7 – *Clothing*   58

    Unit 8 – *Housing*   63

    Unit 9 – *Occupations*   68

    Unit 10 – *Community*   72

Supplementary Work Sheets   77

Preface

This workbook has been designed by teachers of beginning ESL students. It is aimed towards students who have some degree of literacy and does not address preliterate skills. To be successful with this book, students should have a small oral vocabulary and a knowledge of our alphabet.

The main objectives of Survival English is to teach the most basic functional English patterns to these students. The teaching consists of many small steps that are simple, direct, and repetitive. Because of this, a few of the dialogues will not be conversationally functional. However, the book will provide a vocabulary and structure background in which new knowledge can be integrated.

Theoretically we agree that beginning students should have generous time to develop listening skills before being expected to produce language. However, the need exists to teach literacy as soon as possible along with oral skills, and as adults, these students want to read and write immediately.

Included in each unit is a variety of exercises to reinforce the oral patterns and to teach listening, speaking, reading, and writing. Reading and writing are introduced after the student has mastered oral patterns. This book is based on the theory that students learn to speak English by listening, speaking, reading, and writing, in that order.

OBJECTIVES

1. To teach the most basic functional language patterns in survival situations.

2. To teach language patterns and vocabulary in a systematic and controlled manner.

3. To develop reading and writing skills based on what the student can produce orally.

4. To provide survival information and coping skills necessary for adult living.

SURVIVAL ENGLISH

INTRODUCTION

Survival English, Book 1 is arranged into ten units: *Personal ID, General, Family, Health, Transportation, Food, Clothing, Housing, Occupations, and Community.* Survival topics are listed in the Contents. Essential vocabulary is listed at the beginning of each unit.

Each unit has a series of dialogues representing survival situations. The dialogues are structurally controlled. Following each dialogue are exercises to reinforce patterns from the dialogues. These include literacy practice with work sheets, charts, and paired activities. Each unit has multiple visuals demonstrating the dialogues. Each unit also contains a reading passage that is followed by literacy exercises. For maximum effectiveness, all exercises need to be practiced orally first.

Coping Skills Chart	1. Personal ID	2. General	3. Family	4. Health	5. Transportation	6. Food	7. Clothing	8. Housing	9. Occupations	10. Community
1. Socializing	x	x		x	x	x	x	x	x	x
2. Expressing states of being	x			x		x		x		
3. Asking about feelings	x			x		x		x		
4. Apologizing										x
5. Attracting attention		x		x	x	x				x
6. Introducing people									x	
7. Correcting	x		x	x	x	x		x		
8. Asking for information	x	x	x	x	x	x	x	x	x	x
9. Giving information	x	x	x	x	x	x	x	x	x	x
10. Asking for location		x	x		x					
11. Giving location		x		x						
12. Giving classroom directions		x								
13. Following classroom directions		x								
14. Identifying		x	x	x	x				x	x
15. Expressing emotion, hope approval, gratitude, sympathy		x	x	x	x	x		x	x	
16. Expressing understanding						x				
17. Explaining			x	x		x		x	x	
18. Requesting one to do something								x	x	
19. Seeking permission				x	x		x	x		x
20. Giving permission							x	x		
21. Giving instructions				x	x		x			
22. Following instructions				x	x		x			
23. Giving complements							x			

Coping Skills Chart (cont'd)	1. Personal ID	2. General	3. Family	4. Health	5. Transportation	6. Food	7. Clothing	8. Housing	9. Occupations	10. Community
24. Giving invitations							x			
25. Accepting invitations							x			
26. Asking for clarification						x	x		x	x
27. Inquiring about likes and dislikes						x	x			
28. Inquiring about needs and wants						x				
29. Expressing intent							x			
30. Answering the telephone				x				x		x
31. Asking to speak to someone								x		x
32. Identifying oneself				x				x		
33. Reporting needs				x	x					x
34. Reporting a problem				x				x		x
35. Warning					x					
36. Giving directions					x	x				
37. Requesting assistance				x	x					
38. Offering assistance							x			x
39. Suggesting a course of action				x			x			x
40. Instructing someone in a course of action				x	x			x		x
41. Inquiring about capability									x	x
42. Expressing desire, want, or need						x	x		x	x

The above coping skills are found in dialogues in the units that are marked.

Scope and Sequence Chart

	1. Personal ID	2. General	3. Family	4. Health	5. Transportation	6. Food	7. Clothing	8. Housing	9. Occupations	10. Community
1. How is/are___? He's ___.	x	x		x	x			x		x
2. What?	x	x	x	x	x	x	x		x	x
3. Yes/No question with is/are	x		x	x	x		x	x	x	x
4. Subject pronouns: I, you, he, she, it, we, they	x	x	x	x	x	x	x	x	x	x
5. Possessive pronouns: my, her, his	x	x	x	x	x		x	x	x	x
6. How old?	x		x							
7. Where?		x	x		x		x		x	x
8. Please	x	x		x		x			x	x
9. What time?		x			x					
10. Present continuous			x	x	x	x	x	x	x	x
11. How much?				x	x	x	x	x		x
12. Objective pronouns: him, her				x			x			
13. Who?			x							
14. Yes/No questions with do/does				x	x	x	x	x	x	x
15. How many?				x				x		
16. Why? Because ___.			x	x		x	x	x	x	
17. What's the matter?				x				x		x
18. What's wrong?				x				x		
19. When?				x			x	x		
20. Were/was				x			x		x	x
21. Yes/No questions with can					x		x	x	x	x

Scope and Sequence Chart (cont'd)	1. Personal ID	2. General	3. Family	4. Health	5. Transportation	6. Food	7. Clothing	8. Housing	9. Occupations	10. Community
22. Too					x	x	x	x	x	x
23. Or						x	x	x	x	
24. And						x	x	x		x

The above words, phrases, and language patterns are found in dialogues in the units that are marked.

TEACHING THE VISUALS

Each unit has one or more pages of visuals. Each visual is numbered. The teacher is encouraged to use the visuals in creative and innovative ways. The primary use, of course, is to teach the vocabulary. The teacher can do this effectively by making transparencies of the visuals and teaching with the overhead projector. Class-size flash cards can be made by projecting the visuals onto paper from the overhead projector, and tracing the images onto 8" x 11" flash cards. Use felt pens to add color. With these large visuals the teacher can drill new vocabulary, review old vocabulary, play games, develop stories, etc.

To teach the vocabulary, show the visual and say the word that the picture represents. Using the weather visuals as examples, follow the sample exercise:

Teacher	Class
Hold up the rainy visual and say, *"Rainy."* Reinforce pronunciation and repeat, *"Rainy."*	*"Rainy."*
Pick up next visual, which shows hot weather. Say, *"Hot."*	*"Hot."*
Hold up the visual of rain. Say, *"Rainy."*	*"Rainy."*
Show visual of hot weather. Say, *"Hot."*	*"Hot."*
Repeat, *"Hot."* Hold up next visual. Say *"Cold."*	*"Cold."*

Add new vocabulary words, but constantly review the words previously introduced. The visuals are numbered so the teacher can ask, *"What's number 1?"*. Class responds. Teacher asks, *"What's number 2?"* Class responds.

The next activity with the weather, or any visual, is to use the vocabulary in the context of the dialogue. The teacher drills the vocabulary in the language pattern. Hold up the visuals or point to them on the overhead, and say, *"It's rainy."* Class repeats, *"It's rainy."* After the class correctly repeats the names of the visuals, point to or hold up each visual and have the class respond without the teacher's prompting. Then the teacher develops the dialogue by adding, *"How's the weather?"* Class responds according to the picture presented. Hold up the next picture and ask, *"How's the weather?"* Repeat for all the visuals.

Next practice *yes* questions. Teacher asks, *"How's the weather?"* Class responds, *"It's sunny."* The teacher asks, *"Is it sunny?"* Teacher leads class to say, *"Yes, it is."* Repeat this step with all the visuals. Then add *no* questions. Hold up the visual and ask, *"Is it cold?"* Teacher cues class and says, *"No, it isn't."* Class repeats, *"No, it isn't."* The teacher will frequently have to cue the students with the correct answers. Also point out to the class how the voice is raised (inflection) when asking a *yes/no* question. Have the class practice listening and recognizing whether or not the sentence is a question or a statement. Use the visuals as much as possible to avoid false interpretation.

The visuals are also useful in developing literacy. Make flash cards of the words for each visual. Hold up the picture and the corresponding word. Read the word, spell the word, count the letters, and underline the syllables. Hand out both visual flash cards and word flash cards among the students and call out a word. The two students who have matching flash cards must stand or hold them up. You can divide the class into teams and play for points.

Use the visuals and the word flash cards to cue the literacy work sheets. If the worksheet practices *yes/no* questions, review them in the manner previously mentioned before the students write in their books. After the students have completed the exercises, read them aloud or ask individuals to read them. Have the class pair up and read the exercises to each other.

Use the visuals to practice the exercises demonstrated by the charts. Tape the class-size visuals onto the blackboard and draw the lines to simulate the book exercise. *Do not* proceed with exercises in the book until the class has mastered the vocabulary and is familiar with the oral language patterns.

TEACHING THE DIALOGUES

The dialogues are the core of the book and require the most amount of class time. We have suggested seven steps for teaching the dialogues. For the first five steps, the students keep their books closed.

> **STEP 1:** The class listens as the teacher and an aide read the dialogue several times. If there is no aide, the teacher may read A and B parts of the dialogue but in a manner clear to the students that there are two people talking. The teacher and the aide act out the situation in the dialogue as much as possible and use props to demonstrate the meaning.

> **STEP 2:** The teacher introduces new vocabulary by showing pictures, using props, pantomiming the specific words, etc. Teacher pronounces new vocabulary words. Class repeats. Teacher writes new words on the board and reads them. Class reads the words. The teacher can review old language patterns and substitute the new vocabulary with drills.

> **STEP 3:** Begin orally drilling the dialogue with the new vocabulary in known patterns. Introduce a new sentence or phrase from the dialogue. Begin with phrases if the sentences are too long for the students. Teacher says sentence or phrase; class repeats. Listen for pronunciation difficulties and review frequently to correct them. Strive for the students' understanding of the dialogue, correct pronunciation, and memorization of the dialogue. The class repeats the entire dialogue, sentence by sentence, or phrase by phrase after the teacher. When applicable, use the visuals to transform the drills. For example, the teacher holds up the picture of downtown and asks, *"Where are you going?"* The class answers, *"I'm going downtown."* Practice and A and B parts of the dialogue by dividing the class into two sides. Men can be B, women, A; and vice versa. Pair practice the dialogue by tables, rows, or any other division in

the classroom. When the students are comfortable and successful, and repeating the dialogue after the teacher, go on to Step 4.

Note: This entire process has been done orally, with no reading of the dialogue at all.

STEP 4: Begin by writing the dialogue on the board. Write only one sentence at a time. Read the sentence in the same manner as the class began to speak it. Begin with the new vocabulary that the class has seen at the beginning of the lesson. The teacher reads the phrases; the class reads after the teacher. Use a pointer to guide their eyes and point out the words. The teacher reads the entire sentence; the class reads after the teacher. Write the next sentence on the board and continue as with the first sentence. Occasionally review the first sentences. Take time to underline syllables, pronounce words, emphasize the final consonants, and correct pronunciation difficulties. Continue to write the entire dialogue on the board one sentence at a time. If the students have begun to commit the dialogue to memory in the third step, it will now be reinforced in their memory and the words easily recognized.

STEP 5: Students practice speaking the dialogue individually. The dialogue is on the board or a transparency carried over from Step 4 when the class was reading it. The students are now going to speak individually without reading the dialogue. The teacher may wish to cover the dialogue, but the students generally feel more secure talking if the dialogue is visible. Encourage the students to look at each other while speaking. But so as not to threaten the class, let them peek at the board for visual cues if necessary. Help out the students if they are struggling; and if a student does not wish to speak in front of the class, respect his or her wish. More learning will occur if the students are comfortable, rather than afraid.

STEP 6: Students can now open their books and read the dialogue. Give them enough time to make notes or translate the new vocabulary. Have the class underline the new vocabulary words. They may want to write a translation on the page or on the vocabulary page at the beginning of each unit. Have the whole class read the dialogue a few times before asking students to read to a partner in the A/B manner. Encourage them to read the dialogues and, when applicable, substitute the vocabulary found at the bottom of many of the dialogues.

STEP 7: Review the dialogue on following days.

LITERACY PRACTICE WITH THE WORK SHEETS

In the student's book there are literacy work sheets on the bottom of the dialogue pages or on the following pages. If you notice students having trouble focusing on a particular part of the page, use an index card to cover all but necessary material. Before any of the work sheets are attempted, drill the patterns orally. Use the visuals you have enlarged to demonstrate vocabulary. Write sample exercises on the board. Read them together as a class. Students read the exercises after the teacher. They answer orally, and the teacher corrects the students if they are wrong. Then the students work in their books.If the students are familiar with most of the words, the literacy exercises will be a great reinforcement. While the class is writing in their books, circulate around the room to help those who may be having more difficulty than others. Duplicate an exercise on the board or overhead, and, when the class has completed their exercises, quickly review the answers by filling in the duplicated copy on the board. Encourage the class to correct their papers from the board. Read the exercise sentence by sentence, and have the class repeat. The class can pair practice the exercise by reading with a partner.

CHARTS

There are several different charts in the book, all of which are to encourage conversation based on familiar patterns. The charts help to develop speaking, reading, and organizing skills. They can also test whether or not students have mastered vocabulary items and are able to construct sentences orally without a lot of written cues. The student must remember the vocabulary from the previous units as well as the current one.

Present the chart by drilling orally. Students' books are closed. Use the visuals as much as possible to simulate on the board the chart in the book. Hold up a picture or draw figure on the board. Ask the figure's name (any name will do, but simple names have been used repeatedly in the charts so the students will not be burdened with learning many different names).

Teacher	Class
"What's her name?"	"Ann."
"Her name is Ann."	"Her name is Ann."
"Who is she?"	"She's Ann."
"Is she Ann?"	"Yes, she is."

Hold up a flash card on which is written the word "single."

Teacher	Class
"Is Ann single?"	"Yes, she is."
"No, she isn't single." "Is she single?"	"No, she isn't single."

*Tape or write the word, **single** on the board, simulating the chart.*
*Hold up a flash card that says, **widowed**.*

Teacher	Class
Is Ann widowed?"	"Yes, she is." or "No, she isn't."

*(Some may answer **yes**, some **no**. (The teacher guides the answer to match the charts.)*

Teacher	Class
"Yes, she is. She's widowed."	"Yes, she is, She's widowed."

*Tape or write the word, **widowed** next to the word, **single** on the board. Place a check mark under the word **widowed** on the board. Hold up the next flash card which says, **divorced**.*

Teacher	Class
"Is she divorced?	"No, she isn't. She's widowed."

*Tape or write the word **divorced** beside the word **widowed** on the board. Hold up a flash card that says **married**.*

Teacher	Class
"Is Ann married?"	"No, she isn't. She's widowed."
"Who is widowed?"	"Ann is widowed."

The teacher then adds the next row in the same manner. After the second row is finished, review the first row. The teacher can ask the questions out of sequence if the class is comprehending the material. The third and following rows are added slowly. Only after the class can correctly answer your questions should they open their books and pair practice the patterns. Circulate around the room to listen, help and encourage. The next day review the chart. When the class is finished practicing the oral patterns, they may read and write answers to the questions that follow. If there are no questions in the student book, see the notes on the appropriate page in this guide for examples. Always review orally written exercises after the class has finished them. Some charts have blanks, requiring the students to ask each other information. The students ask the appropriate question and write the answer in the correct space.

Use the charts to generate student writing. Students can write sentences based on the vocabulary learned by using the chart.

READING PASSAGES

Develop the reading passages as slowly as possible. Do not assume that the students have conquered English, but rather that they are reinforcing their speaking, reading, and writing skills. Make a copy of the visual shown on the passage page, draw a sketch on the board, or bring in another picture that illustrates the basic idea. Ask leading questions to obtain the story. As the students answer the questions, write them on the board to make the story. Follow this sample activity from the Personal ID unit.

Teacher	Class

Hold up a visual and ask the class.

"Who are they?"..."Tom and Mary."

No, they aren't Tom and Mary.
They are Sue and Joe.

"What's his name?" ...."Joe."

"His name is Joe." ...."His name is Joe."

"What's her name?"..."Her name is Sue."

"Who's he?" ...."He's Joe."

"Who's she?" ...."She's Sue."

Teacher	**Class**

*Write **Sue** and **Joe** on the board.*

"Are they married?" ...."Yes, they are."

"Yes, they are." ...."Yes, they are."

"They are married." ...."They are married."

*Write **are married** after Sue and Joe.*

"How is Joe?".."He's fine."

"He's fine. He's happy." ...."He's happy."

"How's Sue?"..."He's happy."

"No, Sue is a woman. She's happy."....................................."She's happy."

"How are they?..."They're happy."

"They're happy."

*Write **"They're happy."** on the board.*

Read the passage thus far.
"Sue and Joe are married. They're happy."

Ask a student, "What country are you from?"..........................."I'm from Vietnam."

"What country is Joe from?" ...."He's from Vietnam."

"No, he's from Mexico.".."He's from Mexico."

"What country is Sue from?" ...."She's from Mexico."

"Good, she's from Mexico."
Write on the board, "They're from Mexico." ....They're from Mexico."

Read the entire passage.

"Sue and Joe are married." ...."Sue and Joe are married."

"They're happy." ...."They're happy."

"They're from Mexico." ...."They're from Mexico."

The story is now on the board. The class has developed it from your leading questions. Ask the questions from the book and have the students answer them orally before they open their books and do the exercises. After the class reads the questions, they can write the answers. When the class has finished writing the answers, divide the class into two sides and have them read the questions and answers. Write the questions on the board. The teacher may write the answers or have the students come up and write on the board. Encourage students to correct their work.

ACTIVITIES AND GAMES

1. Use the visuals and corresponding flash cards to create games that teach vocabulary and language patterns. Put the visuals from the current unit on the blackboard. Have the class repeat the words after you, as you tape them on the board or wall. Take away the pictures leaving the words alone on the board, and have several students come and try to place the pictures correctly with the words. This activity can also be done in reverse.

2. Divide the class into teams. Give each team a set of flash cards written in a different color so you can tell the teams apart. Tape up pictures, and have the teams race to tape all their flash cards below the correct picture.

3. Tape all pictures from a unit on the board. Have students from various teams come forward. All the students need to do is race and point to the correct picture as you call out its name.

4. Teach location by placing the visuals around the room. Put the skirt next to the shoes on one wall, the pants next to the socks on another wall. Ask the class, "Where's the skirt?" Class looks around the room and responds, "It's next to the pants," etc.

5. Have students come to the front of the class and pick out a picture of a state of being. Write on a sentence strip, "Mai is fine today," or "Lee is cold today." Use the state of being the student picked out along with their name. Tape the sentence strips to the wall. Later, ask, "How is Mai?" or "Is Lee cold?" etc. These can be changed or added to daily.

6. Use the food and clothing units to review money. Have the students place the visual in front of them so they can write on it. The teacher dictates, "The grapes are 69 cents." The class looks for the picture of the grapes and writes on it, "69 cents." After you have dictated an amount of money for all the pictures, test their correctness by asking, "How much are the grapes?"

7. The AEIOU game on page 59 is a modified version of bingo. The squares are blank so the teacher can run off several copies and use them frequently. In the beginning of the semester have the class write in numbers or the alphabet one letter or number per square. You can give "free" spaces to simplify the game or limit the vocabulary. The object of the game is for the students to get five in a row and then call out, "AEIOU." Later in the semester have the students write in the names of the food, clothing, or transportation items. A point of caution is to limit the vocabulary so there will be many AEIOUs. The teacher will be calling out the words that the students have written. Tell the students to write in only the words from specific pages and then use only those words.

8. Reviewing the alphabet is fun if you divide the class into teams and have them race to the front of the room and write the complete alphabet on the board. Very few students do it perfectly.

9. Review the vocabulary items from the crossword puzzles before the students fill in the squares. Demonstrate to students that the words can go only top to bottom or left to right.

10. The purpose of this activity is for the students to practice writing personal information such as their address, birth date, social security number, etc., and then to recognize their own information when it is read back by the teacher. Ditto them, and cut into small squares, each a form asking for that information. For the sake of time, ask for two or three pieces of information per activity. Put all small papers containing student's information into a paper bag. Take a paper out, read the information and have the student whose information was read say, "It's mine." From here on the activity can vary. Those students who are called may go home first, get a small prize, get a point for their team, etc. This is a good activity to do once a week throughout the semester.

TEACHING THE PICTURE PAGE

Ask students, *"What do you see?"* Have students name the objects they know in the picture. It is easier to begin listing nouns than verbs. Students can write the words on the picture or number the picture and list the words on another page. After you have generated the names of many of the items, ask, "What is happening in the picture?" You can practice the present continuous tense, "The boy is fishing," or you can write a story about the picture. Ask *yes/no* questions from the picture, "Is the boy fishing?" and *wh* - questions, "Where is he fishing?" Use your imagination to develop oral and written language skills.

TOTAL PHYSICAL RESPONSE (TPR)

Total Physical Response refers to giving a command to students and having them respond physically. For example: say to the class, "Pick up your pencil." The class responds by each student picking up his or her pencil. The class makes no vocal response. The rationale for this method is that students understand spoken English before they are able to speak. This method utilizes and reinforces those listening and comprehension skills.

We suggest that you set aside five minutes during each class session for a TPR activity. You can give commands such as: "Stand up. Look down. Take out a paper. Write your name on the top. Walk to the door. Take out your driver's license. Pick up your chair." etc. Make this a fun relaxing time and be creative with your commands. Perhaps a particularly verbal student would like to give commands. Vary the commands to coincide with the current new vocabulary being learned. For example, while studying clothing, bring in a basket of clothes and give commands to several students (or an individual student). "Take the shirt. Put the shirt on the table. Find the hat. Put the hat on the teacher. Take the jacket. Give the jacket to a friend." etc.

This activity can be used with many pages of _Survival English 1_. Here are a few examples. *After page 5*: Line large visuals of the new words up on the board. Point to the first row of students and say, "Stand up. Walk to the board. Point to "cold." Pick up "tired." Give "tired"to the teacher. Go back to your seats." Continue with the second row of students using different commands. As you give commands, you may need to act them out yourself so students understand. *After page 18*: Give a blank paper to each student: "Pick up your paper. Put your paper under your chair. Put your paper on your head. Put your paper on your table (desk). Pick up your pencil. Write your first name on the top. Write your last name on the bottom. Write your middle name next to your first name. Turn your paper over. Give your students commands you know they understand. Vary the commands and occasionally add new ones. Do a similar writing TPR *after page 20* and add SS number, telephone number, and address. *After page 35*: "Pick up your chair (pencil, pen, book, paper, etc.) Walk to the chalkboard. Point to the window (clock, pencil sharpener). Open the window (door). Close the window (door). These are just a few suggestions for using TPR with _Survival English 1_. TPR activities are unlimited. Have fun with them.

USING THE SUPPLEMENTARY WORK SHEETS

At the back of this teacher's manual you will find black-line masters for individual student use. Many of the pages are designed to be used after particular pages in the student book. If that is the case, the page number is given at the bottom of the supplementary work sheet. If no page number is given at the bottom of the supplementary work sheet, you may use these pages where you feel they best fit in with your routine. Many of the unmarked work sheets may be used many times — for example, "Listen and write." Some of the work sheets will work for advanced students who finish early, some are printing practice, some are grammar, some are additional reading selections. We encourage you to make work sheets of your own. Thank you for using _Survival English 1_.

SURVIVAL ENGLISH (Page by Page)

UNIT 1 – PERSONAL ID

PAGES 1 AND 2

The vocabulary is listed under the dialogue in which it is first used. The students may wish to write notes or translations next to the words.

PAGE 3 — PERSONAL 1

*Warm-up – Demonstrate this greeting with as many people and as many times as necessary. Act it out by walking toward someone and, as you meet, using this social greeting. After doing this, teach the you/I pronouns, pointing to a person for **you** and to yourself for I.*

> **DIALOGUE** – See *"Teaching the Dialogues."* Review this greeting at the beginning of each class with your students.

> **_Note:_** Direct students to write their names on the line at the top of the page. Demonstrate that the information goes on the line, not under it or beside it. You may need to remind students daily to fill in the line. Make large visuals to use in drills. See *"Teaching the Visuals."*

PAGE 4

Warm-up – These visuals are provided as cues for the subject pronouns and are to be used throughout this text. The students should be familiar with these pronouns.

ACTIVITY: Point to a man *(he)*, a woman *(she)*, you /I, we, and *they*. Repeat orally many times until students are familiar with them. Introduce the written word that corresponds. Match the word to the picture. See *"Teaching the Visuals"* for more teaching ideas. Teach the *you /I* together, gesturing with your hand. These two are used together in the text.

> **_Note:_** Review these subject pronouns daily, cuing with the visuals. Begin to teach these words as sight words and spelling words.

PAGE 5

*Warm-up – Review the **you/I** question and answer formation. Have one outgoing student demonstrate these states of being with props such as gloves for cold, sitting in a chair, demonstrating tiredness, etc. You are repeating orally only: "He's/She's hot, He's/She's tired," etc. Then have other students come up and show **they**. Hold up the visual that matches the state of being they are demonstrating. Stress the* *he/she difference. Eventually, cue the adjective with the visual.*

ACTIVITY: See *"Teaching the Visuals."* Have students write the correct sentence on the line in the appropriate box. Read as a class and as pairs.

PAGE 6 — PERSONAL 2

*Warm-up — Review the state of being visuals and pronouns with the verb **to be** (she's, he's, etc.).*

DIALOGUE – See *"Teaching the Dialogues."*

ACTIVITY: Tape the visuals on the board and write the words on the board. Have students match visuals and words by drawing lines connecting the word to the visual. They will do this on their page after they are successful on the board.

> *Note:* Mix up visuals and flash cards and have students match the visual to the word. Act out feelings and see how quickly students can identify them. Direct students to write their names on the line at the top of the page.

PAGE 7

*Warm-up — Review the subject pronouns. Review the states of being with the verb **to be**.*

ACTIVITY: Reproduce the boxes at the top of the page on the board and orally drill the sequence from one box to the other, pointing to the words as you go. Repeat until students are comfortable. Make some mistakes: "How is she? He's fine." See if students can hear the error. Write these questions on the board, leaving blanks for the answers. Read the questions with students, filling in the blanks orally. Repeat until students can finish the page alone. See *"Literacy Practice with the Work Sheets."*

> *Note:* Half of the students read the first question; half read the answer. Continue reading all questions and answers.

PAGES 8 AND 9

Warm-up — Review orally the questions and the answers.

ACTIVITY: Read as you write the complete question on the board, "How is she?" Read as you write the answer on the board, "She's fine." When the class has mastered the sentences orally, guide them to the written exercise. After they have completed the exercise, read it as a group and in pairs.

PAGES 10 AND 11 — PERSONAL 3

Warm-up — Review states of being and subject pronouns, using flash cards with words and visuals.

DIALOGUE – Hold up visual of fine and ask "Fine?" Solicit a *yes* from students. Hold up visual of *tired* and repeat, "Tired?" Solicit a *yes* from students. Continue through visuals in similar manner. Repeat the exercise, asking the complete question: "Is he cold?" Solicit the complete response: "Yes, he is." See *"Teaching the Dialogues."*

ACTIVITY: Cue with visuals; ask the question. Do not read yet. Tape the visuals on the board and write the question, including the blanks. Read the sentences and cue the answers. Continue until students can finish the page alone. See *"Literacy Practice with the Work Sheets."*

PAGES 12 AND 13 — PERSONAL 4

*Warm-up — Review state of being visuals, subject pronouns, and **yes/no** questions.*

DIALOGUE – Hold up visual of fine and ask "Fine?" Solicit a *yes* from students. Hold up visual of *sad* and ask, "Tired?" Solicit a *no* from students. Continue through visuals in similar manner, concentrating on the *no* response. Repeat the exercise, asking the complete question: "Is he cold?" Solicit the complete response: "No, he isn't." See *"Teaching the Dialogues."*

ACTIVITY: Using visuals, ask the questions and have students respond orally. Tape up visuals, and write the sentences, filling in the blanks orally and cuing from the words in the boxes. Repeat until students can complete the page on their own. See *"Literacy Practice with the Work Sheets."* Correct students' work. Afterwards, read the questions and have students read the answers.

PAGE 14

Warm-up — Review making positive and negative answers.

ACTIVITY: Hold up visual, asking the complete question. Solicit the complete response, "No, he isn't." or "Yes, he is." Practice the exercise orally. Read the sentences, cuing the answers with visuals. When students are successful, have them finish the page alone. Read in pairs or groups when completed.

PAGE 15 — PERSONAL 5

Warm-up — Review making negative answers.

DIALOGUE – Ask an outgoing and obviously happy student if he or she is sad. Drill the pattern: "Are you happy? Yes, I am. Are you busy? No, I'm not." See *"Teaching the Dialogues"* and drill the pattern with all visuals of states of being.

ACTIVITY: Read the questions and answers. Have students answer correctly about themselves.

PAGES 16 AND 17 — PERSONAL 6

Warm-up – Review names "Ann Lee" and "Bob Jones," using visuals. Practice reading these names from flash cards. Point out the two names: first name and last name, or family name. Some cultures assign names differently than the United States. For example, in Laos a married woman retains her family name. Explore this for your students. Review **his** *and* **her.**

DIALOGUE – See *"Teaching the Dialogue."*

ACTIVITY: Using visuals or students in the class, ask the questions, "What's his first/last name?" Duplicate the words in the boxes on the board: *his, her, first, last,* and cue the answers using these words. Tape the visuals on the board, and write the sentences next to them. Read the sentences and orally fill in the blanks until the students can complete the exercise on their own. See *"Literacy Practice with the Work Sheets."* Help students write their first and last names on numbers 5 and 6. Read sentences. This will introduce Personal 7.

PAGE 18 — PERSONAL 7

Warm-up – Review the first and last names of Ann Lee and Bob Jones. Review the subject pronoun visuals **you/I.**

DIALOGUE – See *"Teaching the Dialogues."* Teach the *your/my* as it corresponds to you/I. Show the way it is used: *my name, my pencil, my book, your name, your pencil, your book.* Guide the students through writing their first and last names. Be sure the class understands the American concept of first and family names. In some cultures they name differently.

> *Note:* Fold a 4" x 8" card. Have students write their first name on one side (indicate by a 1) and their last name on the on the other side (indicate by a 2). This card is displayed on their desks for several weeks. Frequently ask students: "What's your first name? What's your last name? Spell it. Hold up your last name. Show me your last name." Ask class, "What's his name? What's her name?" Begin a large chart in the class with personal information: telephone number, address, state, marital status, children, zip code, city, personal information, etc. Use your judgment as to recording the personal information, because although some cultures may not mind, others may.

PAGE 19 — PERSONAL 8

Warm-up – Review information on Bob Jones. Teach the visuals at the bottom of this page: address, social security number, telephone number.

DIALOGUE – See *"Teaching the Dialogues."* Some students don't have telephones. Teach them to say, "I don't have a telephone," or simply, "No telephone."

ACTIVITY: Tape visuals on the board and write the corresponding words in random order beside the visuals. Have students match visuals to words by drawing connecting lines from word to visuals. Continue to match until students are recognizing word and picture.

PAGE 20 — PERSONAL 9

*Warm-up – Review first name, last name, address, telephone number, and social security number, using visuals to cue students. Review **your/my.***

DIALOGUE – See *"Teaching the Dialogues."* Assist students in filling in blanks with their own information. Have them write this same information inside their name cards for quick reference.

ACTIVITY: Have students practice reading the same words in capitals or small letters before they fill in the blanks with their personal information.

PAGE 21 — PERSONAL 10

Warm-up – Review personal information from previous dialogues.

DIALOGUE – See *"Teaching the Dialogues."* Assist students in filling in the blanks, and have them add this personal information to their name cards for quick reference. Practice the dialogue with relevant material.

> **Note:** Spend as much time as necessary with students in oral questioning to review personal information. Have them question each other.

PAGE 22

Warm-up – Review all personal information covered so far both orally and by having students read the word from flash cards.

ACTIVITY: Have students fill in the top half of the page. Drill the fill-in sentences orally. Then write the nine sentences on the board leaving the blanks. Read these with students having them fill in their own information orally. When they seem to be able to handle reading the information, have them proceed to fill in the blanks. See *"Literacy Practice with the Work Sheets."*

Note: Have individual students read aloud the sentences.

PAGE 23

Warm-up — Review the personal information of Bob Jones. Hold up each piece of information and determine what it is: address, city, state, etc.

ACTIVITY: Do the matching exercise on this page several times on the board. Hand out flash cards to students with the personal information of Bob Jones and the personal information words on them. Have students find the matches by circulating and asking other students. Practice until students understand and can finish this page on their own. Have them fill in the bottom half of the page individually.

PAGE 24 — PERSONAL 11

Warm-up—Review Bob Jones' personal information and each student's personal information. Review subject pronouns (I, you, he, she).

DIALOGUE – See *"Teaching the Dialogues."* Assist students in filling in their personal information. It is helpful if either the students or the teacher brings in maps of the students' various countries so that the spelling of the cities can be checked for accuracy. Some students may not have lived in a city. Using *countryside* will help them complete the question.

Note: If you are filling in a class chart of personal information, you may want to add this information to it.

PAGE 25

Warm-up — Some students won't understand the concept of a world map. Some will however, and those will enjoy locating places pertinent to their experiences.

ACTIVITY: Use a large world map and identify your city, state, and country. Students can find their native countries and cities. Students can draw lines from their birthplace to their current city via all the cities or countries they have lived in.

Note: The teacher can demonstrate who has traveled the farthest, over more water or land, by holding up the different maps. A globe showing valleys, mountains, water masses, etc., is most helpful. Some students may not be from cities. Teach them to say, "I'm from the mountains," or another appropriate answer.

PAGE 26

Warm-up – Review previous dialogues.

ACTIVITY: See *"Charts."* Develop chart line by line. Afterwards ask questions: "What's her address? What's Bob's zip code? What's her name? What's his telephone number?" Have students ask a partner: "What's your name? What's your address? What's your zip code? What's your telephone number?" Students write in their partners' answers.

> **Note:** On the next day, you can make a work sheet of some of the questions asked orally.

PAGE 27 — PERSONAL 12

Warm-up – Review the personal information for Bob Jones and for each student. Review the months of the year and ordinal numbers 1 – 30.

DIALOGUE – See *"Teaching the Dialogues."* Help students fill in their own birth dates and age in the blanks. Practice dialogue with relevant information.

ACTIVITY: Encourage students to circulate around the room, asking questions of other students as they fill in the blanks.

PAGE 28 — PERSONAL 13

Warm-up – Display some pictures of families showing husband and wife. Indicate that they are married. Review dialogues 3, 4, and 5.

DIALOGUE – See *"Teaching the Dialogues."*

ACTIVITY: Question students: *"Is he married?"* Display the visuals and ask the questions. Reproduce the two boxes on the board: *"Yes, he/she is,"* etc. Write the questions on the board. The students fill in the blanks orally cuing from the boxes. Students complete the exercise by writing in the blanks. See *"Literacy Practice with the Work Sheets."*

> **Note:** Have the women read the questions and the men read the answers, or any combination, to practice reading.

PAGE 29 — PERSONAL 14

Warm-up – Review dialogues 3, 4, 5, and 13.

DIALOGUE – See *"Teaching the Dialogues."* Have students fill in the blank with their own personal information.

ACTIVITY: Practice the exercise orally. When students are comfortable answering orally, let them fill in the blanks. Have students read their answers aloud.

PAGE 30

Warm-up – Review states of being, marital status, and where students are from.

ACTIVITY: See *"Reading Passages."*

PAGE 31

Warm-up – Review married, divorced, widowed, single, and dialogues 13 and 14.

ACTIVITY: See *"Charts."* The class may write the answers to the questions on another day.

PAGE 32

Warm-up – Review all personal information both orally and in written from flash cards.

ACTIVITY: Depending upon your class level, you may want to do this activity with the class. A new concept here is the vertical writing. Show students that left to right is okay and that top to bottom is okay, but not right to left or bottom to top. Show them how the cue pictures help locate the word. See *"Activities and Games."*

UNIT 2 – GENERAL

PAGES 33 AND 34

The vocabulary is listed under the dialogue in which it is first used. The students may wish to write notes or translations next to the words.

The dialogues, exercises, and vocabulary in this unit are designed as supplemental material for the other units. They are based on spiral concepts that take time to develop and need constant reinforcement. For example, money can be reviewed where appropriate in the clothing, food, transportation, etc. units . We suggest that you spend some time every day on this unit in addition to continuing with other units. You may begin this unit concurrently with the first unit, Personal ID.

PAGE 35

Warm-up – Point to objects in the room. Direct the class to point to or touch objects in the room.

ACTIVITY: See *"Teaching the Visuals."* The class can write the word on the picture after they recognize the word in written or oral form. Tape flash cards on the objects in the room. Have the class point to or touch the objects as you say them. Using the visuals, ask the class *"What's number 6?"* Class responds, *"It's a book."*

PAGE 36 — GENERAL 1

Warm-up – Review vocabulary from General visuals. Introduce the prepositions. Students review the vocabulary by physically responding to such commands as "Pick up the book," "Put the pencil on the book," etc.

DIALOGUE – See *"Teaching the Dialogues."*

ACTIVITY: Place items around room and ask students, *"Where's the _____?"* Students answer accordingly. Ask students where the vocabulary items are in the book.

PAGE 37

ACTIVITY: Review the previous dialogue, all the prepositions, and the visuals from page 35. Orally drill the pictures on page 37, asking students where the items are. Reproduce the boxes on the board or on an overhead. Orally drill the correct response until students can successfully complete the exercise on their own. Pair students up and have them practice the question and response: *"Where's the pen? The pen is ____ the table."*

PAGE 38

ACTIVITY: Review the previous dialogue, all the prepositions, and the visuals from page 35. Orally drill the statements from the picture. Have students select the appropriate response from the prepositions written on the board. Orally drill the correct response until students can successfully complete the exercise on their own.

PAGE 39

ACTIVITY: See *"Teaching the Visuals."* Use a student to demonstrate the commands as you give them. Say, *"Go,"* and have a student walk away. Say *"Open the door,"* and have the student demonstrate. Use the verbs with many objects; *"Open the door, the window, the book,"* etc. You can command the entire class to open their books, stand up, sit down, etc. When the class comprehends the commands, you can duplicate this page and cut up pictures. Hand them out to one third of the students. They can each have two or three pictures. They circulate around the room and instruct other students, who don't have pictures, to demonstrate one of the action verbs they have. Example: tell students, *"Open the book."*

PAGE 40

Warm-up – Use this page to reinforce verb visuals from the previous page. Review command form.

ACTIVITY: See *"Literacy Practice with the Work Sheets."*

PAGE 41— GENERAL 2

Warm-up – Review previous visuals and commands.

DIALOGUE – Give the command, and students respond physically. Review until students understand. Write the commands on the board, one at a time, reading as you write. Practice reading from the board before reading from the book. Read a number and students respond physically. Read commands in a random order and have students say which number you have read.

ACTIVITY: Display one pencil, several pencils, one book, several books, etc. Make sure students understand that singular is one and plural is 2, 3, 6, 100, etc. Don't use the terms *singular* and *plural.*

PAGE 42

Warm-up – Review visuals and classroom objects.

ACTIVITY: Hold up one pencil and say, *"pencil."* Hold up two or more pencils and say *pencils*. Demonstrate with as many objects as possible. Have the students say either *pencil* or *pencils* depending on how many you hold up. Write the correct word on the board, and point out the final *s* for plurals. When students have mastered the activity orally, they can proceed to the work sheet. As with other English-language concepts, there are many exceptions to the rule, but at this level we don't mention plurals like *man - men* unless a student asks. These are taught later.

PAGE 43

ACTIVITY: This is the second crossword puzzle. Students may not understand the concept of words going top to bottom as well as left to right and the idea of one letter per square. Using the cue pictures, solicit the correct word from students and guide them in getting started. Another helpful, but very difficult concept, is the idea of crossing out each word on the list as it is used. See *"Activities and Games."*

PAGE 44

ACTIVITY: This page should be referred to often. There are many ways to use it.

1. Counting by 1s: 1, 2, 3, 4, etc.
2. Counting by 10s: 10, 20, 30, etc.
3. Counting by 5s: 5, 10, 15, 20, etc.
4. Counting by 2s: 2, 4, 6, 8, etc.
5. Call a number; students find it and point to it.
6. Group students in pairs. One student says a number and the other student finds it.
7. Dictate numbers to be written by students on a sheet of paper numbered from one to ten.

Orally count together as a class. Stop and allow the students to say the next number in the sequence. Do this with individual students who you know understand the concept. Put number sequences on the board and have students orally fill in the blanks then write them in until they can complete the book exercise alone.

> *Note:* The teen numbers are especially difficult to master. Spend more time on these. Cut up individual sets of 11–20. Students can hold up the number that is called. The same can be done for the 10s, (10, 20, 30, etc.) Contrast 13 with 30, 14 with 40, 15 with 50, etc.

PAGE 45

ACTIVITY: Have students use this page to practice reading and writing numbers.

PAGE 46 — GENERAL 3

*Warm-up – Review **what** questions.*

DIALOGUE – Drill, drill, drill. See *"Teaching the Dialogues."*

ACTIVITY: Demonstrate that the days can be abbreviated. Bring in a calendar on which the abbreviations can be seen.

PAGE 47 — GENERAL 4

*Warm-up – Review General 3 and questions with **what**. Make flash cards of days and months to use for drills.*

DIALOGUE – Use hand gestures to help demonstrate yesterday, today, and tomorrow. See *"Teaching the Dialogues."*

ACTIVITY: Write the seven days on the board. Point to the word Monday. Say, *"Tomorrow is _____."* Continue practicing orally until the class understands. Have class complete sentences.

PAGE 48 — GENERAL 5

Warm-up – Make flash cards of the days of the week and months. Drill, drill, drill.

DIALOGUE – See *"Teaching the Dialogues."* Demonstrate that the date always has three parts: the month, the day, and the year. Have a place in the room to display the date, and make this part of the daily routine. Practice writing the days of the week and the months in the blanks. Use flash cards with the days and months. Use these for games, drills, and review.

ACTIVITY: Demonstrate that the months can be abbreviated. Using abbreviations on flash cards, have the class say the word. Ask class how many letters the short form has. Demonstrate the short form has three or four letters for the word.

PAGE 49

ACTIVITY: Review the months, the calendar concept, and the prepositions before and after. Write the months on the board. Reproduce the 12 sentences on the board and have individual students come up and fill in the blanks. Practice orally until students can proceed alone.

PAGE 50

Warm-up – Review days, months, and counting.

ACTIVITY: Use this calendar to practice ordinal numbers. Ask students: *"What day is the 14th?, What's the last day of the month? What's the first day of the month? How many Sundays in the month?"* Have students circle the date as the teacher dictates. Have students write the complete word for the day of the week above the abbreviation.

PAGE 51

Warm-up – Review days of the week and months of the year with flash cards.

ACTIVITY: As a class make a calendar on the blackboard. Have students fill their calendars out for the appropriate month. When finished, ask questions such as: *"What day is November 3? What is today / yesterday / tomorrow?"* Depending on the class level, you can introduce: *this week, last week, next week.* Do a similar calendar at the first of each month.

PAGE 52

Warm-up – Review days, months, and ordinal numbers.

ACTIVITY: Teacher says date,— for example, "June 15th." Students circle June 15 on the calendar. Say twelve dates, one for each month. Afterwards ask students, *"What day is June 15th?"* Students respond, *"It's Wednesday."* Etc.

PAGE 53 — GENERAL 6

Warm-up – Review "How are you?" and the states of being.

DIALOGUE – See *"Teaching the Dialogues."* Since the weather changes daily, you can use this dialogue every day for good practice.

ACTIVITY: See *"Teaching the Visuals."*

> *Note:* Locate other weather pictures in magazines and use these to reinforce the idea of rain, clouds, etc. An activity might be to sort out all cloudy pictures and put them under the correct heading. Students could be encouraged to look through magazines themselves and locate examples of particular kinds of weather. Print the weather words on flash cards and match with visuals. Ask about the weather in their native countries.

PAGE 54

Warm-up – Review weather pictures, words, and the accompanying dialogue from the previous page.

ACTIVITY: See *"Literacy Practice with the Work Sheets."*

> <u>**Note:**</u> Have students report the weather daily. Ask students about weather in their native countries again.

PAGE 55 — GENERAL 7

Warm-up – Review reading numerals 1 – 60. Introduce, "Excuse me," as a function of socializing.

DIALOGUE – See *"Teaching the Dialogues."* Use a large clock for demonstration. Begin telling time by using the hour hand only. Add the minute hand. Practice reading hours and half hours, then the quarter hours.

ACTIVITY: Demonstrate how to make a clock face on the board. Have students write in the numbers on their clocks, cut out the clock hands, and secure with a brad. The teacher says, *"It's 10:00."* The students move the hands to 10:00 and hold up their clocks. The teacher can quickly see if students can hear the time and can reproduce it on the clock.

> <u>**Note:**</u> Review telling time and reading time from the clock every day. Educational supply stores carry individual plastic clocks for students to manipulate as you direct.

PAGE 56

Warm-up – Review telling time. We suggest teaching students to read time as digital — "eleven fifteen" rather than "a quarter past eleven is easier.

ACTIVITY: Have students show each of these times on their clocks. Write the list of times that appear at the bottom of the page, on the board. Set the class clock for each of these times in turn, and have students locate the digital time that matches. Repeat until students are secure enough to finish the page alone. Correct pages. Have individual students read the time as you call the number of the clock in the book.

PAGE 57

Warm-up – Review the clock face, the hour hand, the minute hand, and telling time.

ACTIVITY: Using a large clock, demonstrate the times shown on the small clocks in the book. Have students read them. In items 7–12 in the book, have students read each of the times aloud. Make the class clock match the times. Students complete the page after a lot of oral practice.

PAGE 58

Warm-up – Review the clock face and telling time.

ACTIVITY: The students make 12 clocks. Teacher says, *"Number 1, it's 12:00."* Continue for all 12 clocks. Afterwards, ask class, *"What time is number 6?"* Students answer. This page can, of course, be duplicated and used often.

PAGE 59

Warm-up – Review letters of the alphabet.

ACTIVITY: See *"Activities and Games."*

PAGE 60

ACTIVITY: Have students cut along the dotted lines and keep the letters in an envelope. There are numerous activities for these letters.

1. Call a letter; students hold it up.

2. Say a word; students hold up the beginning or end consonant letter.

3. Say the isolated sound; students hold up the letter or group of letters that represent the sound.

4. Students pick out any letter or group of letters and ask a partner.

5. Students pick out any letter or group of letters, and ask a partner to say a word beginning with that letter.

6. Students can spell words from beginning units, *his, her, my, it, is, I,* etc.

7. Students put letters in alphabetical order.

   Note: Constantly review the sounds of the alphabet.

PAGE 61

ACTIVITY: Review the alphabet in order orally. As you practice it, stop and allow the students to say the next letter in the sequence. Do this with individual students who you know understand the concept. Put letter sequences on the board and have students orally fill in the blanks then write them in until they can complete the book exercise alone.

PAGE 62 — GENERAL 8

Warm-up – Money presents the same difficulties for students as addition and subtraction. Almost all students understand the idea that coins and bills stand for some value and that one dime is worth the same as any other dime, one dollar is worth the same as any other dollar, etc. They usually understand the concept of making change: that is, the idea of paying an amount that is more than the total of the item you are purchasing and getting money back. However, don't assume even these basic notions and make these concepts clear as you come to them. Following are some items to keep in mind as you teach money.

1. Money is an extension of counting and, as such, we don't suggest you begin to teach money until numbers have been mastered (the reading and writing of 1-100). Also, don't attempt the addition of money until basic addition has been mastered.

2. Identify the name and value of the four basic American coins. Make sure the students know the distinction between the name and the amount. In many cases, they need to know how to read the words, too.

3. Money should be taught slowly. You could easily spend two weeks on this one page. Do a little each day, but do it every day.

4. Begin by identifying the name of the coins. Get a money kit at your local school supply store. (It's an excellent investment.) Have students hold up the penny, hold up the quarter, hold up one cent, hold up twenty-five cents.

5. Dictate amounts of money to students. Ask them to write the numerals, including the decimal point and cent sign, where applicable.

ACTIVITY: Draw samples of the coins on the blackboard. Practice matching the word, to the coin, to the amount. After students understand the new items, have them match in their books.

PAGE 63

Warm-up – Review counting by 10s and 5s.

ACTIVITY: Show samples of coins and have class identify their value. Have students write in their books after they can answer correctly orally.

PAGE 64

Warm-up – Review coins and amounts.

ACTIVITY: Practice each line orally first. Ask students how many pennies are in a nickel, etc.

PAGE 65

Warm-up – Review counting by 10s and 5s.

ACTIVITY: There is a big gap between this page and the previous one. You may need to make additional work sheets with more practice in counting amounts of money. Do a lot of practice with counting just pennies, just dimes, or just nickels.

> <u>*Note:*</u> Have students take out the change they currently have with them and count it.

PAGE 66

Warm-up – Review reading amounts of money and counting change.

ACTIVITY: Using their individual play money, have students show which coins they would use to buy the items pictured. Have students then complete the page alone.

34

UNIT 3 – FAMILY

PAGES 67 AND 68

The new vocabulary is listed under the dialogue in which it is first used. The students may wish to write notes or translations next to the words. This is always one of the students' favorite units. It can also be sad, because so many families have been split up or had members die.

PAGE 69 — FAMILY 1

Warm-up – Introduce family relationships: mother, brother, husband, etc. An activity that clarifies these relationships is to form "families" from students in the class-room. Make large printed flash cards, using the words, **mother, father, son,** *etc. Pick a man and give him a sign saying man. "He needs a wife." Find a woman and give her a* **woman** *card. Give her a* **wife** *card as well, and give the man the* **husband** *card. "They have a son." Pick a student and give him the* **son** *card. Build up the family and the relationships until the family encompasses the entire class. Each time you add people, establish the relationship. "Is he a son? Is she a mother/a wife?" Introduce mother-in-law, aunt, uncle, etc. You can also make two families and, as they grow, have their children marry and demonstrate in-laws as well as the American custom of wives taking their husband's name.*

DIALOGUE – See *"Teaching the Dialogues."*

> <u>*Note:*</u> Ask students if other students are sisters, brothers, friends, etc.

PAGE 70

*Warm-up – Review family relationships and the words that describe them. Add the new words introduced on this page (***grandmother, aunt,** *etc.) Make flash cards of the words and have students match the gender to a visual of a man and woman taped on the board.* **Friend** *and* **cousin** *can obviously be either male or female. Practice reading the eleven sentences together orally as a class, having students fill in names of their own relatives.*

PAGE 71 — FAMILY 2

Warm-up – Review "Where is your pencil? Where is your book?" etc.

DIALOGUE – See *"Teaching the Dialogues."*

ACTIVITY: Orally practice the questions and responses that go with the visuals. Practice in pairs until students can complete the exercise alone.

PAGE 72 — FAMILY 3

Warm-up – Review the previous dialogue.

DIALOGUE – See *"Teaching the Dialogues."*

ACTIVITY: See *"Teaching the Visuals."* Duplicate sets of these verbs and hand one picture to each student. Have students stand up in turn and act out the verb. . Teacher: *"What's he doing?"* Student: *"He's cooking."* Teacher: *"Is he cooking?"* Student: *"Yes, he is."* Continue around the room. Have students write the subject and the verb on the picture.

PAGE 73

Warm-up – Review verbs: **cleaning, taking care of, cooking,** *and* **studying.**

ACTIVITY: See *"Literacy Practice with the Work Sheets."* Read aloud when class is finished. Have students correct their papers.

PAGE 74

Warm-up – Review verbs: **cleaning, taking care of, cooking,** *and* **studying.** *Review making negative answers.*

ACTIVITY: See *"Literacy Practice with the Work Sheets."* Read the questions and answers aloud after students are finished.

PAGE 75 — FAMILY 4

Warm-up – Review Family dialogues.

DIALOGUE – See *"Teaching the Dialogues."*

ACTIVITY: These are questions to ask students after the dialogue: *Do you have children? How many children do you have?* Does he/she have children? *How many children does he/she have?* See *"Literacy Practice with the Work Sheets."*

PAGE 76 — FAMILY 5

Warm-up – Review previous dialogues.

ACTIVITY: See *"Literacy Practice with the Work Sheets."* If students have no children, they may respond, *"No, I don't. I have no children."* to the questions.

PAGE 77 — FAMILY 6

Warm-up – Review: "How old are you? How old is he/she?"

DIALOGUE – See *"Teaching the Dialogues."*

ACTIVITY: You may wish to make a larger version of this chart with spaces for every student. They can fill in their own information or it can be done as a class activity. Students listen as the questions are asked of other students. The smaller chart may be filled in by students circulating around the room collecting information on their own.

> *Note:* Questions to ask students: *"Do you have children? How many children do you have? How many sons? How old are they? How many daughters? How old are they? How many children are in school? How many children are at home?"*

PAGES 78 AND 79

Warm-up – Review Dialogues 5 and 6.

ACTIVITY: See *"Literacy Practice with the Work Sheets."*

PAGE 80 — FAMILY 7

*Warm-up – Introduce **Mr., Mrs., Miss,** and **Ms.** Find out names of the local elementary and secondary schools.*

DIALOGUE – See *"Teaching the Dialogues."*

ACTIVITY: Oral questions to use with students: *"How many children do you have? How many children are in school? What school? What grade? Who is the teacher?"* If additional reinforcement is needed, a class chart can be made listing students' names, how many children they have, names of children's schools, names of children's teachers, and grades children are in.

PAGE 81 — FAMILY 8

Warm-up – Review Dialogue 7. Teach the name of your school. Remind students of your name.

DIALOGUE – See *"Teaching the Dialogues."* Students fill in appropriate name of their school and the teacher's name.

ACTIVITY: Students orally answer the three questions until they can read and writ the answer.

> **Note:** Oral questions from the dialogue to ask students: "Are you a student? What's the name of your school? Who is your teacher?"

PAGE 82 — FAMILY 9

Warm-up – Review family and relationship names. Review: "Do you have brothers? How many? Do you have sisters? How many?" Etc.

DIALOGUE – See *"Teaching the Dialogues."* This is the first time for the structure *who / because*. Plan enough practice using substitutions so this structure becomes familiar: "I'm going home." "Why?" "Because I'm busy."

> **Note:** Review the states of being and add **excited**.

PAGE 83

Warm-up – Review relationships. "Do you have brothers, sisters, sons, daughters, a grandmother, a grandfather? How many?"

ACTIVITY: See *"Literacy Practice with the Work Sheets."*

> **Note:** Put these questions on slips of paper. Hand one or two out to half the students. They circulate, asking these questions of other students.

PAGE 84

Warm-up – Review unit dialogues.

ACTIVITY: See *"Reading Passages."*

PAGE 85

Warm-up – Orally review all of this information. Hand out flash cards to students with printed information words on them: **name, zip code, from,** *etc. These students walk around the room and ask this information from other students.*

ACTIVITY: See *"Literacy Practice with the Work Sheets."* Read the sentences one at a time. Call on individual students to answer the questions. Depending on the level of your class, have students fill in the sentences one at a time or all at one time. Draw your family on the board to demonstrate what is expected in the rectangle. If students are willing. hold up the drawings to share with the entire class. They may be interested in seeing how large a family their classmates have aside from their artistic talents.

PAGE 86

Warm-up – Review Dialogues 3, 4 and 5.

ACTIVITY: See *"Reading Passages."*

PAGE 87

Warm-up – Review names of family members.

CROSSWORD PUZZLE – See *"Activities and Games."*

UNIT 4 – HEALTH

PAGE 88 AND 89

The vocabulary is listed under the dialogue in which it is first used. The students may wish to write notes or translations next to the words.

PAGE 90

Warm-up – Students stand up, teacher commands, students act: "Touch your head, touch your chest, touch your arm," etc. This is not only a good way to drill these nouns but also a good break in classroom routine. Variations of this can be done daily. "Wiggle your fingers, wiggle your ears," etc. Once the body parts are learned, progress to: "Put your right hand on your left shoulder." As the body part is pointed to, have students refer to this page, locate the word, and spell it. Using beginning consonant sounds as clues, read the words.

> **Note:** Teacher quickly sketches a large outline of a body on butcher paper. Print up large flash cards of the body parts. Have students tape the name on the body part.

PAGE 91 — HEALTH 1

*Warm-up – Review the verb **to be** using the states of being from the first unit.*

DIALOGUE – See *"Teaching the Dialogues."* Substitute other body parts for stomach. "My head hurts; my back hurts; my chest hurts;" etc.

ACTIVITY: Review body parts on flash cards before having students draw lines matching the part to the word.

> **Note:** Review states of being including **sick**.

PAGE 92

Warm-up – Review: "What's the matter?" and "My head hurts." Review parts of the body.

ACTIVITY: See *"Literacy Practice with the Work Sheets."*

PAGE 93 — HEALTH 2

Warm-up – Review: "Do you have children? Do you have a pencil?" etc. See "Teaching the Visuals" for use with the visuals.

DIALOGUE – See *"Teaching the Dialogues."*

> *Note:* From magazines in the room, see if students can locate some pictures depicting the four new problems. Ask students about any health problems they have.

PAGE 94

*Warm-up – Review **do** and **does** questions with **yes/no** answers. Emphasize the negative response.*

ACTIVITY: See *"Literacy Practice with the Work Sheets."*

> *Note:* Have students ask questions of other students as they take the visuals around the room. Students ask, "Does he have a fever?" Another student answers, "No, he doesn't. He has a broken arm."

PAGE 95

ACTIVITY: See *"Reading Passages."*

PAGE 96

VISUALS – See *"Teaching the Visuals."*

> *Note:* Have students write complete sentences matching pictures with verbs.

PAGE 97

Warm-up – Review "What's he doing?" and verbs from the previous page.

ACTIVITY: See *"Literacy Practice with the Work Sheets."*

PAGE 98 — HEALTH 3

Warm-up – Review family relationships. Review states of being and "I have a _____." Review previous health dialogues.

DIALOGUE – See *"Teaching the Dialogues."*

Note: Practice using telephones in the classroom. Often the local telephone company has a system they loan out to schools for practicing calls. The 911 is an emergency number in use in large cities and may not be applicable to your area. Please check.

ACTIVITY: Teacher solicits the action by asking, *"What's the matter? What's he/she doing? Where are they going?" etc.* Continue orally only. These sequence pictures can be duplicated, cut up, and put in correct order by students or matched with sentence strips.

PAGE 99 — HEALTH 4

Warm-up – Review: "What's the matter/what's wrong?" and visuals from Dialogue 2. Review previous health dialogues.

DIALOGUE See *"Teaching the Dialogues."*

ACTIVITY: Practice reading thermometers. Indicate which temperature does not indicate illness and which ones do. This may be new information, so don't forget to teach what's normal. Draw a large thermometer on the board. Use a chalk line to demonstrate the fever rising.

Note: Cut up a class set of thermometers, each indicating different temperatures. Have students circulate with these thermometers, practicing the dialogue.

PAGE 100 — HEALTH 5

Warm-up – Review personal information. Have some health forms to hand out to students while practicing the dialogue.

DIALOGUE – See *"Teaching the Dialogues."*

ACTIVITY: Refer to a student in class. Review his personal information, using the information given here. Write it on the board. Copy a chart on the board. Proceed to fill in the "new-patient" form, using the student's personal information. Note the concept of putting a check as opposed to writing in the information. Have students fill out the form, using their own identification.

PAGE 101 — HEALTH 6

Warm-up – Review: "What's the matter?" health visuals, and previous dialogues. Review necessary personal identification.

ACTIVITY: Indicate that the students are to fill in only their information in blanks on the prescription.

> *Note:* Set up a pharmacy in the room. Ask the students to fill in their names and addresses. Bring in bottles with regular and child-proof caps so the class can practice opening them.

PAGES 102 AND 103

*Warm-up – Both the phrases, **when** and **how much** are new. Take as much time as necessary to teach these concepts. Bring in a real teaspoon, tablespoon, and prescription bottles, if possible.*

ACTIVITY: See *"Literacy Practice with the Work Sheets."*

> *Note:* Pretend several students are sick and need medicine. Give each of those students a medicine bottle containing chocolate chips or small candies. Write the bottle directions on the board. Example: take two pills in the morning. Practice answering "how much?" and "When?" Have some class members direct others in the proper dosage of medicine, while those students follow the directions.

PAGE 104 — HEALTH 7

Warm-up – Review family relationships: son, daughter, sister, brother, "What's his name? "What's her name?" Review previous health dialogues.

DIALOGUE – Have students fill in their names and their child's name in the proper boxes. See *"Teaching the Dialogues."*

> *Note:* Practice the dialogue, using play telephones.

ACTIVITY: See *"Literacy Practice with the Work Sheets."*

PAGE 105

*Warm-up – Review Health Dialogue 1 and body parts. Review the verb **need**.*

ACTIVITY: See *"Literacy Practice with the Work Sheets."*

PAGE 106 — HEALTH 8

*Warm-up – Review the **why/because** structure and "I need a checkup." Review telling time.*

DIALOGUE – See *"Teaching the Dialogues."*

ACTIVITY: Have students fill in the appointment information after you have reviewed it orally.

PAGE 107 — HEALTH 9

*Warm-up – Review the **why/because** structure. Review **yes/no** questions with the states of being: "Is she sick? No, she isn't."*

DIALOGUE – See *"Teaching the Dialogues."*

ACTIVITY: The students listen and follow the teacher's directions: "Pick up your pencil. Draw two eyes. Draw one nose. Draw two ears. Draw a mouth. Draw hair. Draw a neck. Draw two arms. You may make the drawings as complicated as you wish. You may have a good student come to the board and draw on the board as the others do at their seats.

PAGE 108

Warm-up – Review all necessary vocabulary.

ACTIVITY: See *"Reading Passages."* Ask students if they have an appointment. Write and read their story on the board or transparency. Write questions on the board for class to answer orally.

PAGE 109 — HEALTH 10

*Warm-up – Review Health 1. Explain that we tell a time change by the tenses of verbs. **Am, are** and **is** occur in the present tense, or today, while **was** and **were** occur in the past. Review General Dialogue 4.*

DIALOGUE – See *"Teaching the Dialogues."*

ACTIVITY: Reproduce the two boxes on the board and drill orally. See *"Literacy Practice with the Work Sheets."*

PAGE 110

ACTIVITY: Have students cover the sentences. Ask questions of students cuing the answers from the picture, "Who is he? What's the matter? What's his mother doing?" etc. Do orally several times. Write responses on the board or on sentence strips. Read sentences in the correct order. Mix up the sentence strips and have students put them in order. Students open books and read in their books. Students can number or cut out the sentences and practice putting them in sequential order. Students can also write the story in the present continuous tense: "taking his temperature," "calling the doctor," etc.

PAGE 111

Warm-up — This is the first time the book has used the past tense of **have**. **Is/ was** *was introduced in General 4. Review the* **is/was** *to reinforce the idea of* **past tense**. *Don't use the term* **past tense** *with the students unless someone asks.*

ACTIVITY: Reproduce the two boxes on the board and drill orally. Take some time here to use the past tense with other situations. Reproduce the sentences on the board and drill orally until the students can complete the exercise on their own. See *"Literacy Practice with the Work Sheets."*

PAGE 112

STORY – See *"Reading Passages."* Review Health Dialogues and stress the past tense.

PAGE 113

ACTIVITY: See *"Teaching the Picture Page."*

PAGE 114

CROSSWORD PUZZLE – See *"Activities and Games."*

PAGE 115

The vocabulary is listed under the dialogue in which it is first used. The students may wish to write notes or translations next to the words.

PAGE 116

VISUALS – See *"Teaching the Visuals."*

> <u>*Note:*</u> Take students outside and review types of transportation seen on the street. Point out license numbers, crosswalks, traffic lights, stop signs, no parking signs, etc. Identify types of transportation found in magazines, newspapers, etc. If space permits, begin a class bulletin board of pictures of the various transportation modes. Have students match the names on flash cards with the modes.

PAGE 117 — TRANSPORTATION 1

Warm-up – Review vocabulary and visuals from previous page.

DIALOGUE – See *"Teaching the Dialogues."* Use the visuals from the following page to demonstrate the additional ways of getting to school. Ask students how they come to school.

PAGE 118

Warm-up – Review Dialogue 1.

VISUALS – See *"Teaching the Visuals."* Students can write the sentences under the correct picture.

PAGE 119

*Warm-up – Review "How **do/does?"** questions, and **yes/no** questions. Review the transportation visuals. Review Dialogue 1.*

ACTIVITY: See *"Literacy Practice with the Work Sheets."* Practice the exercise with a city or location the students know. They may not be familiar with L.A. but you can substitute another city.

PAGE 120 — TRANSPORTATION 2

Warm-up — Review Dialogue 1, **yes/no** *questions with do and telling time.*

DIALOGUE – See *"Teaching the Dialogues."* Fill in the telephone number of the local bus company and the location of your school. In drilling this dialogue, substitute other methods of transportation and other destinations.

PAGE 121

ACTIVITY: See *"Charts"* in the front of this guide. Here are some suggestions for questions with the chart: How does Bob Come to School? How does Bob go downtown? How does Ann come to school? How does Ann go downtown? How do they come to school? How do they go downtown? Does Bob take the bus to school? Does Bob drive a truck downtown? Who takes the bus? Who rides a bicycle? Does Ann ride a bicycle? Does Ann drive a van downtown? Does Ann take the bus? Does Ann drive a truck? Do they ride motorcycles downtown? Do they ride bicycles? Etc.

PAGE 122

VISUALS – See *"Teaching the Visuals."* Arrange to visit the places near your school. Tape visuals on the walls in the room. Tell the students to go to the bank, go to the hospital, etc. They walk to the pictures. As they are walking toward the picture, ask where they are going. Using the transportation mode visuals, instruct students: "Go to the park on the bicycle." They will choose the bicycle visual and take it to the park visual.

PAGE 123 — TRANSPORTATION 3

Warm-up — Review **where's, it's** *and prepositions.*

DIALOGUE – See *"Teaching the Dialogues."*

ACTIVITY: Students can draw a line from the word to the picture, or they can rewrite the word correctly next to the picture. Ask students, *"What's number 1? What's number 6?"*

PAGE 124 — TRANSPORTATION 4

Warm-up — Review "Where are you going?", "I'm going... ," and **yes/no** *questions with the verb* **to be.**

DIALOGUE – See *"Teaching the Dialogues."* Fill in the fare on the local bus.

ACTIVITY: See *"Literacy Practice with the Work Sheets."*

PAGE 125 — TRANSPORTATION 5

Warm-up – Review **yes/no** *questions with verbs* **to do** *and* **to be.**

DIALOGUE – See *"Teaching the Dialogues."*

ACTIVITY: See *"Literacy Practice with the Work Sheets."* Set up a bus in your room, (chairs in a row for seats, driver, coin box, etc.) and role play these dialogues.

PAGE 126

Warm-up – Review visuals of places and ways of transportation.

ACTIVITY See *"Literacy Practice with the Work Sheets."*

PAGE 127

ACTIVITY: Use the pictures to teach the verbs: (1) Wait for the bus. (2)Get on the bus. (3) Put in the money. (4) Sit down. (5) Pull the bell. (6) Stand up. (7) Get off. Students can respond physically as the teacher says, *"Stand up"* or *"Pull the bell."* Later practice, *"What's he doing?"*, *"He's waiting for the bus,"* and all the verbs in the present continuous. Have individual students give the commands to the rest of the class, using the visuals as cues.

PAGE 128

Warm-up – Review written names of places as seen on the buses.

ACTIVITY: See *"Literacy Practice with the Work Sheets."* Observe actual busses outside the classroom. Ask students where the busses are going.

PAGE 129 — TRANSPORTATION 6

Warm-up – Review "Where's the," **yes/no** *questions with* **to be,** *and prepositions.*

DIALOGUE – See *"Teaching the Dialogues."*

ACTIVITY: Use the map to drill additional locations, i.e., "Where's the bus stop? Where's the hospital?" etc.

PAGE 130 — TRANSPORTATION 7

*Warm-up — Review places, **Where's...?**, and the vocabulary.*

DIALOGUE – See *"Teaching the Dialogues."* The man in the lower right of the map is the starting point. Have students pretend to drive, turn right, turn left, and stop.

ACTIVITY: Reproduce a large map. Use either butcher paper or a transparency. Have one student give directions to a place while another drives a small toy car.

Note: Introduce and teach the word **block** which is used in the map segment.

PAGE 131

Warm-up — Review visuals of places.

ACTIVITY (1) Ask students, *"Where's the hospital?", "Where's the school?", "Is the hospital on the corner?", "Is it on 2nd Street?", "Is it on 1st Street?"*, etc. (2) After students can answer the above, use the following listening and speaking sample. Teacher says, *"It's on 2nd Street. It's on the corner. It's not the church. What is it?"* Students answer, *"It's the school."* Practice this with all the places on the map. (3) Tell students you are at the theater. Have them direct you to the grocery store. They must say *"turn right"* or *"turn left,"* etc. Make a map of the students' immediate environment, perhaps locating a few of their homes and shopping places. Do similar questioning as above.

PAGE 132

Warm-up — Review visuals of places and the street names.

ACTIVITY: Duplicate the visuals of places on page 122. Have students cut these up into individual pictures. Direct the students: *"Put the gas station on 1st Street. Put the bank next to the gas station. Put the school on 3rd Street. Put the bus stop in front of the school."* After all the visuals have been placed, ask students, *"Where's the bus stop?"* They respond and the teacher continues to ask the location of the other places.

PAGE 133

Warm-up — Review visuals of places, "It's on the corner", and "Where's?"

ACTIVITY: See *"Literacy Practice with the Work Sheets."*

PAGE 134

*Warm-up — Review visuals of places, methods of transportation, **who, where,** and* **how.**

ACTIVITY: See *"Charts."* Suggestions for questions: Who goes to the gas station? Is Ann going to the gas station? How does Ann go the gas station? Does Ann drive a car? Does Ann walk? Who goes to the hospital? Who takes the bus? Does Bob go to the hospital? Does Bob take the bus? Does Bob take the bus to the hospital? Where are they going? Are they going to school? Are they riding their bicycles? Are they going to the grocery store? Etc.

PAGE 135 — TRANSPORTATION 8

Warm-up — Review **yes/no** *questions with* **do,** *and the verb* **need.**

DIALOGUE – See *"Teaching the Dialogues."* Emphasize the punctuation marks.

VISUALS – See *"Teaching the Visuals."* Enlarge visuals or copy onto the board. Have students stand, pretend to drive or walk, and obey the signs as you point to or hold them up.

PAGE 136

Warm-up — Review all necessary vocabulary for the story.

ACTIVITY: See *"Reading Passages."*

PAGE 137 — TRANSPORTATION 9

Warm-up — Review **yes/no** *questions with* **do.**

DIALOGUE – See *"Teaching the Dialogues."*

VISUALS – See *"Teaching the Visuals"* and *"Games and Activities."* Make large signs and have students obey the signs as they walk about the classroom. You can do a lot of teaching here. Many students want a driver's license and need much more information than is presented here. The Department of Motor Vehicles booklet is a good place for more ideas.

PAGE 138 — TRANSPORTATION 10

Warm-up — Review **yes/no** *questions with* **to be.** *Review* **how's.**

DIALOGUE – See *"Teaching the Dialogues."* Arrange to have class examine an actual car and its parts. Have students write the word under the picture. Use pictures to review parts of the car.

PAGE 139

ACTIVITY: See *"Teaching the Picture Pages."*

PAGE 140

Warm-up – Review visuals on methods of transportation. Have students write the correct word next to the picture before filling in the puzzle. See "Games and Activities" in the front of this guide.

UNIT 6 – FOOD

PAGE 141

The vocabulary is listed under the dialogue in which it is first used. The students may wish to write notes or translations next to the words.

PAGE 142

> *Note:* When teaching the food unit, use as many examples of the real thing as possible. Bring in different kinds of bread, drinks, etc., as well as magazine and newspaper advertisements of the vocabulary items. You can buy plastic fruit and vegetables in school supply stores or toy stores.

VISUALS – See *"Teaching the Visuals."*

PAGE 143 — FOOD 1

Warm-up – Review vocabulary and visuals from the previous page.

DIALOGUE – See *"Teaching the Dialogues."*

ACTIVITY: Reproduce the chart on the board, taping up the visuals in the appropriate place. See *"Charts."* Suggestions for questions: Do I have milk? Do I need milk? Do I have bread? Do I need bread? Do I have eggs? Do I need eggs? Does he have fish? Does he need fish? Who has milk? Who has fish? Practice questions with all subject pronouns.

PAGE 144

ACTIVITY: Drill the sentences orally, using the visuals as cues. After oral practice, write the sentences on the board, leaving the blanks. Tape the visuals up in the appropriate place. Read the exercise and orally fill in the blanks. See *"Literacy Practice with the Work Sheets."*

PAGE 145 – FOOD 2

*Warm-up – Review the **do** structure ("Do you have children?" "Yes, I do." "No, I don't."), vocabulary, and visuals.*

DIALOGUE – See *"Teaching the Dialogues."*

ACTIVITY: Bring in actual meat stickers to look at. Copy them on the board for the entire class to see. Show what the three different numbers represent. The total is almost always the largest number. It's helpful to bring in a scale to demonstrate pounds.

Reproduce the sticker on this page on the board. Include the blanks to fill in. Orally practice the total price and price per pound. Teach the different names of meat: pork, fish, hamburger, and chicken. Later ask: *"How much is the chicken?" "How much a pound is the chicken?" "How many pounds is the chicken?"*

PAGE 146

Warm-up – Review activity on previous page.

ACTIVITY: Reproduce the meat stickers on this page on the board. Practice reading the total price and price per pound aloud. Teach the different names of meat: pork, fish, chicken. Ask,*"How much is the chicken?"*, etc.

PAGE 147

VISUALS – See *"Teaching the Visuals."*

PAGE 148

Warm-up – Review visuals and vocabulary.

EXERCISE: See *"Literacy Practice with the Work Sheets."* Make flash cards of *Yes* and *No.* Tape the subject pronoun visuals (*she, he, we, they*) and the food visuals on the board. Ask the questions cuing from the visuals. For the answer, hold up a *yes* or *no* flash card and have students respond correctly.

PAGE 149

Warm-up – Review visuals.

ACTIVITY: See *"Literacy Practice with the Work Sheets."* Review the idea of plural and demonstrate various numbers of food items until students understand that any number larger than one has the plural *s.* Tape food visuals on the board and draw blanks next to them. Orally drill with students. Repeat until students can finish the page alone. In reviewing plurals, include parts of the body and items around the room: one finger, four fingers, one pencil, seven pencils.

PAGE 150

Warm-up – Review subject pronoun visuals, food visuals, and the verbs **to go** *and* **to need.**

ACTIVITY: See *"Literacy Practice with the Work Sheets"*. Orally drill the sentences, cuing with the subject pronoun visuals. Write the sentences on the board, leaving in the blanks. Read the sentences, orally filling in the blanks. Repeat until students can complete the page alone.

PAGE 151 — FOOD 3

Warm-up – Review food visuals and vocabulary.

DIALOGUE – See *"Teaching the Dialogues."*

ACTIVITY: Review the names of food items and ask the class, "How much are the grapes?" Write the food words on the board with the blanks next to them. Say the price per pound. Practice until students can finish the activity alone.

> **Note:** Take a trip to a nearby store and identify the *lb.* and *ea.* Bring in the newspaper showing the food ads. Often they have pictures listing the price beside the item.

PAGE 152

Warm-up – Review food visuals and vocabulary. Practice addition.

ACTIVITY: See *"Literacy Practice with the Work Sheets."* These prices are totals, not per pound. Orally question. Read the questions, filling in the blanks orally until the students can complete the page alone.

PAGE 153

Warm-up – Review food visuals and vocabulary.

ACTIVITY: See *"Reading Passages."*

PAGE 154 — FOOD 4

Warm-up – Review vocabulary.

DIALOGUE – See *"Teaching the Dialogues."*

ACTIVITY: Bring in meat and milk containers to show the expiration dates. Ask students the dates on the samples in the book. Write the questions on the board, leaving in the blanks. Read the questions and orally fill in the blanks. Repeat until the students can finish the page alone.

PAGE 155

VISUALS: Act out each of these verbs so the meaning is clear. See *"Teaching the Visuals."* Students can write the complete sentence under each picture, i.e., "He's eating a hot dog."

PAGE 156

Warm-up – Review the visuals of verbs and vocabulary.

ACTIVITY: See *"Literacy Practice with the Work Sheets."* Orally question, cuing by the visuals. Tape the visuals on the board and write the questions, leaving the blanks. Read the questions with students, orally filling in the blanks. Repeat until students can finish the page alone.

PAGE 157 — FOOD 5

Warm-up – Review visuals of food and verbs.

DIALOGUE – Bring in two foods to eat and two drinks to demonstrate the difference between eat and drink. See *"Teaching the Dialogues."*

> **Note:** Bring, or have students bring, snacks. Ask students, "Do you like
> _____ ?" "Are you drinking _____?" "Are you eating _____?"

PAGE 158 — FOOD 6

ACTIVITY: Bring in as many measuring cups as possible to demonstrate. Practice reading and writing the different amounts as they appear on the cups.

DIALOGUE – Practice this dialogue and actually bake a cake or two in your classroom. Read the back of the cake mix. Look for a mix that needs water, eggs, and oil, or adjust the dialogue. Involve as many students as possible in measuring, mixing, pan greasing, etc. Use the last section of the dialogue for commands. Act it out many times so students are familiar with the words before they read. Write each command on a sentence strip and have students put them in correct order.

Note: We found icing not necessary. It's too sweet for most students.

PAGE 159

ACTIVITY: Review measuring cup amounts and vocabulary. Bring in some packaged mixes from the store and try reading the amounts on them. Use a variety of measuring cups brought from home and match them to the pictures on the page.

PAGE 160

ACTIVITY: Review measuring cup amounts and vocabulary. Draw visuals on the board and have students fill in amounts. For the bottom half of the page, have them circulate around the room with visuals, asking each other, "How much?" Practice until students can complete the page on their own.

PAGE 161

Warm-up – Review measuring cups and vocabulary.

ACTIVITY: See *"Literacy Practice with the Work Sheets."* These are actual recipes for items that can be made in class with reconstituted milk and a casserole dish. All the students have liked these recipes. Read each recipe and the questions aloud. Read the questions and orally fill in the blanks. Repeat until students can complete the page alone.

> *Note:* Have students make the recipes in class. Use an electric frying pan for the casserole.

PAGE 162 — FOOD 7

Warm-up – Review vocabulary.

DIALOGUE – See *"Teaching the Dialogues."*

ACTIVITY: Make larger visuals for the food items, including the prices at the bottom. Practice *small, medium, large, regular* and *super.* Practice simple addition with the food items. See *"Literacy Practice with the Work Sheets."*

PAGE 163

Warm-up – Review vocabulary.

ACTIVITY: See *"Reading Passages."*

PAGE 164

ACTIVITY: Dictate prices and have students write them on the items. Have class guess the total cost of the groceries in the cart. List some of the student's favorite foods. See *"Teaching the Picture Pages."*

PAGE 165

Warm-up – Review vocabulary.

ACTIVITY: See *"Activities and Games."*

UNIT 7 – CLOTHING

PAGES - 166 AND 167

The vocabulary is listed under the dialogue in which it is first used. The students may wish to write notes or translations next to the words.

PAGE - 168

VISUALS: See *"Teaching the Visuals."* Ask students: *Do you have socks?, Do you have an umbrella?, Do you have a wallet?, etc.* Ask students: *"What are you wearing? Are you wearing a jacket? Is he/she wearing pants?, Etc.*

PAGES 169 — CLOTHING 1

Warm-up — Review clothing items and **yes/no** *questions with the verb* **to be.**

DIALOGUE – See *"Teaching the Dialogues."*

ACTIVITY: See *"Literacy Practice with the Work Sheets."*

PAGE 170

> *Note:* This page may be used following the previous page as a review or it can be used the same day for more advanced students who can handle the additional writing and reading. The previous page names single items. This page has plurals.

ACTIVITY: See *"Literacy Practice with the Work Sheets."*

PAGES 171 — CLOTHING 2

Warm-up — Review vocabulary, telling time, and clothing visuals.

DIALOGUE – See *"Teaching the Dialogues."* Drill: "I need to buy shoes for my daughter,...pants for my son,... socks for my husband." Etc.

ACTIVITY: See *"Literacy Practice with the Work Sheets."*

PAGE 172

Note: This page may be used after the previous page as a review or it can be used the same day for more advanced students who can handle the additional writing and reading. Write the correct sentence on the board for students who may need to copy.

ACTIVITY: See *"Literacy Practice with the Work Sheets."*

PAGE 173 — CLOTHING 3

Warm-up – Review clothing items.

DIALOGUE – See *"Teaching the Dialogues."* Bring in clothing for students to try on. Determine if the items are too small, too big, or just right. Have students examine their own clothing labels for size.

ACTIVITY: Read labels on this page and write the word for the size they indicate.

PAGE 174 — CLOTHING 4

*Warm-up – Review clothing visuals, vocabulary and past tense of **to be (was/were)**.*

DIALOGUE – See *"Teaching the Dialogues."* Look through newspaper ads and store catalogues to practice reading prices and finding sales.

ACTIVITY: See *"Charts."* Hand out construction paper clothes to half of the class. They ask the other students, "How much is the jacket?" The other students look on the chart and respond, "It was $19.95. On sale, $14.95."

PAGE 175

Warm-up – Review clothing items and vocabulary.

ACTIVITY: See *"Literacy Practice with the Work Sheets."*

PAGE 176

ACTIVITY: Use sheets of construction paper to teach colors. Use the sheets as visuals. See *"Teaching the Visuals."* Hand out crayons to students. They read and follow instructions on the page, coloring in the squares with the correct color. Students then cut out the squares. Teacher says, "Hold up red. Put it down. Pick up yellow. Put it down." etc. The teacher can give as simple or as complicated directions as he or she wants. At a glance, the teacher can see if the students know the colors. More complicated commands are: "Put the green paper in your notebook," or "Give the yellow paper to a friend." Tell students to keep the squares for review.

PAGE 177

Warm-up – Review clothing items.

ACTIVITY: See *"Reading Passages."*

PAGE 178 — CLOTHING 5

Warm-up – Review clothing items and vocabulary.

DIALOGUE – See *"Teaching the Dialogues."*

ACTIVITY: This exercise can be either commands given by the teacher or a reading exercise for students, depending on the level of the class.

PAGE 179

VISUALS: See *"Teaching the Visuals."* Have the class write the correct subject verbs and objects under the pictures.

PAGE 180

Warm-up – Review verbs from the preceding page.

ACTIVITY: Remind students to begin the sentences with capitals. See *"Literacy Practice with the Work Sheets."*

PAGE 181 — CLOTHING 6

Warm-up – Review clothing items, vocabulary, and "Do you have?" questions.

DIALOGUE – See *"Teaching the Dialogues."* Make the situation as realistic as possible by using actual clothing items and receipts.

ACTIVITY: See *"Charts."* Let the class know that most stores require a receipt for a return or exchange.

PAGE 182 — CLOTHING 7

Warm-up – Review clothing visuals, money, and "I want to buy _____" with visuals.

DIALOGUE – See *"Teaching the Dialogues."* This dialogue has some sophisticated concepts. You may need an interpreter to clarify *cash, charge,* and *tax.* The students are familiar with tax *but* not *charge.* Charge cards are very difficult for some of them to comprehend. Practice adding tax to prices of clothing. Subtract that total from amount tendered.

> <u>*Note:*</u> Compute taxes according to your area and fill in the square accordingly.

PAGE 183 – CLOTHING 8

Warm-up – Review clothing items and vocabulary.

DIALOGUE – See *"Teaching the Dialogues."* Give these commands to the students. Act out the commands as much as possible. Have students eventually give the commands, substituting whatever clothing items they wish.

ACTIVITY: Students write the words from the top of the page beside the picture.

PAGE 184 — CLOTHING 9

*Warm-up – Review vocabulary and **yes/no** questions.*

DIALOGUE – See *"Teaching the Dialogues."*

ACTIVITY: Have students orally supply the missing parts. Students fill in the exercise. Students read exercise orally. Write the two sentences on the board, "Ann is going to sewing class. She's making a shirt." Read aloud. Erase the verbs and have students repeat the sentences. Have students fill in the blanks after oral practice.

PAGE 185 — CLOTHING 10

> <u>*Note:*</u> Bring in thread, needles, scissors, material, and buttons to demonstrate. Then have students actually use the materials. Say one direction slowly — demonstrate. Say next direction and demonstrate. See *"Teaching the Dialogues."* Practice orally. Have some students follow the directions given by classmates. Have half the class direct the other half, but only in English, to sew on a button.

ACTIVITY: Students write the word under the picture.

PAGE 186 – CLOTHING 11

Warm-up — Review vocabulary and language patterns.

DIALOGUE – See *"Teaching the Dialogues."* Visit a laundromat if possible. Bring soap and bleach and do a load of laundry if this is new to the students.

ACTIVITY: See *"Literacy Practice with the Work Sheets."*

PAGE 187

Warm-up — Review the clothing visuals.

ACTIVITY: See *"Activities and Games."*

UNIT 8 — HOUSING

PAGE 188

The vocabulary is listed under the dialogue in which it is first used. The students may wish to write notes or translations next to the words.

PAGE 189

VISUALS: See *"Teaching the Visuals."*

PAGE 190 — HOUSING 1

Warm-up – Review vocabulary, **yes/no** *questions with* **to be.**

DIALOGUE – See *"Teaching the Dialogues."* Bring in play phones.

ACTIVITY: See *"Literacy Practice with the Work Sheets."*

PAGE 191 — HOUSING 2

Warm-up – Review **yes/no** *questions with* **do.**

DIALOGUE – See *"Teaching the Dialogues."*

ACTIVITY: See *"Literacy Practice with the Work Sheets."*

PAGE 192

VISUALS: See *"Teaching the Visuals."* Have students look at the visual and supply the correct subject pronoun. Have them write the subject and complete verb on the picture.

PAGE 193 — HOUSING 3

Warm-up – Review **yes/no** *questions with states of being from Unit I and vocabulary.*

DIALOGUE – See *"Teaching the Dialogues."*

ACTIVITY: See *"Literacy Practice with the Work Sheets."* Bring in the housing rental information from the newspaper so the students become aware that such information is available. Teach the abbreviations found in the paper if students are interested,— for example, *br., ba.*

PAGE 194

VISUALS: See *"Teaching the Visuals."* Students can write the word on the picture.

PAGE 195 — HOUSING 4

*Warm-up – Review "I need," **yes/no** questions with **do**, "How much?" and **yes/no** questions with **to be**.*

DIALOGUE – See *"Teaching the Dialogues."*

ACTIVITY: After drilling from the visuals and flash cards, the students draw lines connecting the picture to the correct word.

PAGE 196

Warm-up – Review previous dialogues.

ACTIVITY: Teach the abbreviations for apartment, bedroom, and bathroom. Put the sample ads on the board and identify the abbreviations. Practice the questions orally before students write in books.

> *Note:* "Children O.K." is new.

PAGE 197 – HOUSING 5

*Warm-up – Review **yes/no** questions with **to be**. Also"How many?" "Do you?" and " Can I?"*

DIALOGUE – See *"Teaching the Dialogues."* Take class outside and locate the gas, water and electricity meters for a few houses and apartments in your neighborhood.

ACTIVITY: After drilling from the visuals and flash cards, have the students draw lines connecting the picture to the word.

PAGE 198

Warm-up – Review bedroom, bathroom, living room, kitchen, and furniture items.

ACTIVITY: Draw the four squares on the blackboard. Hand out large visuals of furniture and tell a student to put the sink in the bathroom, the rug in the bedroom, etc. Make extra copies of the furniture visuals and hand out to students. Students then do the same activity as above, in their books. Tell the students to put the chair in the living room, put the dresser in the bedroom, etc. After you have finished placing the furniture, ask students where the items are: *"Where is the chair?" and "Is the chair in the living room?"*

PAGE 199 — HOUSING 6

*Warm-up – Review **how much, when,** and **next.***

DIALOGUE – See *"Teaching the Dialogues."*

ACTIVITY: The activity is a listening exercise. Practice on the board to demonstrate the exercise. Write *utilities* and *security deposit* on the board. The teacher says, *"Number 1, utilities,"* and then circles the word *utilities*. If the class is at a higher reading level, the teacher says, *"Number 1, utilities, $79 a month."* The students write the money figure next to the correct word. After completing the exercise, review by asking the class, *"In number 1, how much are the utilities?"*

PAGE 200 — HOUSING 7

*Warm-up – Review housing visuals, the **why/because** structure, "That's too bad," and **broken** from the Health unit.*

DIALOGUE – See *"Teaching the Dialogues."*

ACTIVITY: See *"Literacy Practice with the Work Sheets."*

PAGE 201 — HOUSING 8

Warm-up – Review "What's the matter?" and "Can you fix it?"

DIALOGUE – See *"Teaching the Dialogues."*

ACTIVITY: See *"Literacy Practice with the Work Sheets."*

PAGE 202 — HOUSING 9

Warm-up — Review "What's wrong?" and verbs **can** *and* **fix.**

DIALOGUE – See *"Teaching the Dialogues."*

ACTIVITY: Fill in appropriate vocabulary words.

PAGE 203

Warm-up — Review **broken** *and the furniture visuals. Demonstrate* **leaking** *and* **stopped up.**

ACTIVITY: See *"Literacy Practice with the Work Sheets."*

PAGE 204

Warm-up — Review "Can I borrow?" and appropriate vocabulary.

ACTIVITY: See *"Literacy Practice with the Work Sheets."*

PAGE 205 – HOUSING 10

Warm-up — Review "What's the matter?", housing vocabulary, days of the week, **next,** *and the* **Can you?** *structure.*

DIALOGUE – See *"Teaching the Dialogues."*

PAGE 206

Warm-up — Review all necessary vocabulary.

ACTIVITY: See *"Reading Passages."*

PAGE 207

Warm-up — Review housing vocabulary and the "Do you have?" structure.

ACTIVITY: See *"Charts."* Continue to practice in paired conversations with students. One student asks the question. The other student responds, *"Yes, I do,"* or *"No, I don't."* The students enjoy the humor of *"Do you have a toilet in your kitchen?"*

PAGE 208

Warm-up – Review "Do you have?" structure and housing vocabulary.

ACTIVITY: See *"Literacy Practice with the Work Sheets."*

PAGE 209 — HOUSING 11

Warm-up – Review **tomorrow,** *the* **why/because** *structure, and* **yes/no** *questions with* **to be.**

DIALOGUE – See *"Teaching the Dialogues."* Teach and drill the names of cleaning supplies.

ACTIVITY: See *"Literacy Practice with the Work Sheets."*

PAGE 210

Warm-up – Review the verb visuals, pronouns, and "What's he/she doing?" with the verbs.

ACTIVITY: See *"Literacy Practice with the Work Sheets."*

PAGE 211

Warm-up – Review housing vocabulary.

ACTIVITY: See *"Reading Passages."*

PAGE 212

ACTIVITY: See *"Teaching the Picture Pages."*

PAGE 213

Warm-up – Review the housing visuals.

ACTIVITY: See *"Activities and Games."*

UNIT 9 – OCCUPATIONS

PAGE 214

The vocabulary is listed under the dialogue in which it is first used. The students may wish to write notes or translations next to the words.

PAGE 215

VISUALS: See *"Teaching the Visuals."* Explore occupations the students had in their countries and the jobs some may have now.

PAGE 216 — OCCUPATIONS 1

Warm-up – Review **what's** *and subject pronouns.*

DIALOGUE – See *"Teaching the Dialogues."*

ACTIVITY: See *"Literacy Practice with the Work Sheets."*

PAGE 217 — OCCUPATIONS 2

Warm-up – Review **yes/no** *questions with verb* **to be.**

DIALOGUES – See *"Teaching the Dialogues."*

ACTIVITY: See *"Literacy Practice with the Work Sheets."*

PAGE 218

Warm-up – Review **yes/no** *questions with* **to be.**

ACTIVITY: See *"Literacy Practice with the Work Sheets."*

PAGE 219 – OCCUPATIONS 3

Warm-up – Review **where** *and* **what.**

DIALOGUE – See *"Teaching the Dialogues."*

ACTIVITY: See *"Literacy Practice with the Work Sheets."*

PAGE 220 — OCCUPATIONS 4

*Warm-up – Review **yes/no** questions with verb **to be** and the **why/because** pattern.*

DIALOGUE – See *"Teaching the Dialogues."*

ACTIVITY: See *"Literacy Practice with the Work Sheets."*

PAGE 221

Warm-up – Review all necessary vocabulary.

ACTIVITY: See *"Reading Passages."*

PAGE 222 — OCCUPATIONS 5

Warm-up – Review "Are you working?"

DIALOGUE – See *"Teaching the Dialogues."*

ACTIVITY: See *"Literacy Practice with the Work Sheets."*

PAGE 223

*Warm-up – Review **who, was** and **is**. The class can give the man and woman names so they can respond with **he/she** or a specific name when answering **who** questions.*

ACTIVITY: See *"Charts."* Suggestions for questions: Who was a homemaker? Who is a secretary? Was she a homemaker? Is she a secretary? Is she a seamstress? What was his job? What is his job? Who was a mechanic? Who is an assembler? What was your job? What is your job? What was her job?

PAGE 224 – OCCUPATIONS 6

*Warm-up – Review "This is ...", **job**, and **looking for**.*

DIALOGUE – See *"Teaching the Dialogues."* Students can fill in the name of a friend in the blanks and introduce them to the class.

ACTIVITY: See "Literacy Practice with the Work Sheets."

PAGE 225

Warm-up – Review the verbs: **want, fill out, return,** and the new vocabulary.

DIALOGUE – See "Teaching the Dialogues."

ACTIVITY: Read the first half of the story aloud to students, and ask the information below the story. Practice orally several times before students fill in the first half of the job application. The students use the information given about Bob Jones to fill in the application. Read the second half of the story to students. Practice the fill-ins orally until students can fill in the second half of Bob Jones' job application on their own.

PAGE 226 — OCCUPATIONS 7

Warm-up – Review **yes/no** questions with **can** and vocabulary.

DIALOGUE – See "Teaching the Dialogues."

PAGE 227

Warm-up – Review all necessary vocabulary to complete the application. Review the dialogues from the Personal ID unit and the Family unit.

ACTIVITY: The student fills in his or her personal information.

PAGE 228 — OCCUPATIONS 8

Warm-up – Review **yes/no** questions with **do** and vocabulary.

DIALOGUE – See "Teaching the Dialogues."

PAGE 229

Warm-up – Review occupation visuals and subject pronouns.

ACTIVITY: See "Literacy Practice with the Work Sheets."

PAGE 230 — OCCUPATIONS 9

Warm-up – Review occupation visuals, **yes/no** *questions with* **to be,** *and time units of a month, a week, and an hour.*

DIALOGUE – See *"Teaching the Dialogues."*

ACTIVITY: Fill in the information from the help- wanted ads orally first. Practice until students can fill in the chart on their own. See *"Charts.*

PAGE 231 – OCCUPATIONS 10

Warm-up – Review **yes/no** *questions with* **can,** *vocabulary, and "What can he do? "*

DIALOGUE – See *"Teaching the Dialogues."*

ACTIVITY: See *"Literacy Practice with the Work Sheets."*

PAGE 232

Warm-up – Review all necessary vocabulary.

ACTIVITY: See *"Reading Passages."*

PAGE 233

Warm-up – Review occupation visuals.

ACTIVITY: See *"Activities and Games."*

UNIT 10 – COMMUNITY

PAGES 234 AND 235

The vocabulary is listed under the dialogue in which it is first used. The students may wish to write notes or translations next to the words.

PAGE 236

VISUALS: See *"Teaching the Visuals."*

PAGE 237 — COMMUNITY 1

Warm-up – Review "Where are you going?", "I'm going …," yes/no questions with to be, opens, closes, and telling time.

DIALOGUE – See *"Teaching the Dialogues."* Drill various opening and closing times and substitute different places. Drill questions at the bottom orally first.

ACTIVITY: See *"Literacy Practice with the Work Sheets."* Reproduce the open/closed times on the board to use with the total class. If possible, visit actual stores in your neighborhood to check for open/closed times in their window.

PAGE 238

ACTIVITY: Review the days of the week. See *"Literacy Practice with the Work Sheets."*

PAGE 239 — COMMUNITY 2

Warm-up – Review "next", "I want… ," what, "Do you have…?", and the verb want.

DIALOGUE – See *"Teaching the Dialogues."* Have each student bring in some ID.

ACTIVITY: See *"Teaching the Visuals."* Bring in samples of various IDs. Have students identify driver licenses and ID cards. Have students take out their own ID and decide what type it is.

PAGE 240 — COMMUNITY 3

*Warm-up – Review vocabulary from Dialogue 2, **please, what,** and "Write your name."*

DIALOGUE – See *"Teaching the Dialogues."* Hand out checks for students to endorse.

ACTIVITY: Fill in the check with the information given. Teach *from* and *to*. Draw a large check on the board and show where the date and amount are. Show students that the amount is in numbers and is also spelled out. Show them how to know who the check is from and who the check is to.

PAGE 241

Warm-up – Review vocabulary from the previous page.

ACTIVITY: See *"Literacy Practice with the Work Sheets."*

PAGE 242

Warm-up – Review checks and vocabulary.

ACTIVITY: Students can practice making out checks to the gas and electric and the telephone companies, etc. Write directions for each check on the board, give students directions orally, or have them write checks to other students in the class.

PAGE 243

Warm-up – Review all necessary vocabulary.

ACTIVITY: See *"Reading Passages."*

PAGE 244 — COMMUNITY 4

Warm-up – Review "Excuse me," the "Do you have...?" pattern, "What do you need?" pattern, and making change.

DIALOGUE – See *"Teaching the Dialogues."* Use play money from a money kit. Set up situations for practice with making change.

ACTIVITY: Review money amounts and addition. Students add up amounts of coins.

PAGE 245 — COMMUNITY 5

Warm-up – Review "Do you have change?" and **yes/no** *questions with* **do.**

DIALOGUE – See *"Teaching the Dialogues."* Look at a pay phone with the class and how it operates.

ACTIVITY: Review money amounts and addition.

PAGE 246 — COMMUNITY 6

Warm-up – Review telephone conversations.

DIALOGUE – See *"Teaching the Dialogues."* Telephones for classroom practice may be supplied by your telephone company.

PAGE 247 — COMMUNITY 7

Warm-up – Review "I'm going to ..." "Can I come?" and "I need to buy ..."

DIALOGUE – See *"Teaching the Dialogues."*

ACTIVITY: See *"Literacy Practice with the Work Sheets."* The visuals used here in the exercise are actually introduced on the following page. Teach them before finishing this page.

PAGE 248 — COMMUNITY 8

Warm-up – Review **yes/no** *questions with* **to be** *"I want to buy," and the word* **next.**

DIALOGUE – See *"Teaching the Dialogues."* Plan a field trip to the post office. Have students fill in the current price of stamps before completing the dialogue.

VISUALS: See *"Teaching the Visuals."* Have students fill in current stamp prices in the dialogue.

PAGE 249

Warm-up – Review **to, from, address, zip code,** *and* **how much.**

ACTIVITY: See *"Literacy Practice with the Work Sheets."* Reproduce the envelopes larger on the board. Orally review the questions before students write the answers in the book.

PAGE 250 — COMMUNITY 9

Warm-up – Review rooms in the house, "I need help," and asking for and giving addresses.

DIALOGUE – See *"Teaching the Dialogues."* Plan a field trip to a fire station. Tell the class about the 911 Emergency Services number if it is in effect in your area.

ACTIVITY: Practice the sentences, cuing from the visuals.

PAGE 251 — COMMUNITY 10

Warm-up – Review telephoning, asking for and giving name and address, as well as Dialogue 9.

DIALOGUE – See *"Teaching the Dialogues."* Bring in substances that are harmful to children: soap, bleach, cleanser, etc.

PAGE 252 — COMMUNITY 11

Warm-up – Review past tense of **to be (was/were)** *and furniture or personal items that are often stolen.*

DIALOGUE – See *"Teaching the Dialogues."*

ACTIVITY: See *"Charts."* Students fill in personal information at the bottom of the page. Students can write sentences for the chart.

PAGE 253 — COMMUNITY 12

Warm-up – Review emergency situations from dialogues, and giving and asking for personal information. Distinguish between a real 911 emergency and just needing to see a doctor.

DIALOGUE – See *"Teaching the Dialogues."* Invite a policeman to visit your room at a time an interpreter will be available. New arrivals to our country are unfamiliar with the laws. You might discuss the penalty for various offenses, i.e., jail sentences.

PAGE 254 — COMMUNITY 13

Warm-up – Review vocabulary and the verb **to be.**

DIALOGUE – See *"Teaching the Dialogues."* Bring in samples of bills and advertisements to examine.

ACTIVITY: See *"Literacy Practice with the Work Sheets."*

PAGE 255

Warm-up – Review all necessary vocabulary.

ACTIVITY: See *"Reading Passages."*

PAGE 256 — COMMUNITY 14

Warm-up – Review questions and answers with **can,** *"How much?", and "Let me."*

DIALOGUE – See *"Teaching the Dialogues."*

ACTIVITY: See *"Literacy Practice with the Work Sheets."* Have students bring in their own bills if they are confused about them.

PAGE 257 — COMMUNITY 15

Warm-up – Review questions and answers with **can** *and* **do.** *Review types of ID.*

DIALOGUE – See *"Teaching the Dialogues."* Depending upon the level of your class, you may want to visit a library. Check ahead to see what is required for students to obtain a library card.

ACTIVITY: Fill in appropriate information and answer the questions.

PAGE 258

Warm-up – Review all the necessary vocabulary.

ACTIVITY: See *"Reading Passages."*

PAGE 259

VISUALS: See *"Teaching the Visuals."* These may be used at any point in the book. Identify as many as possible around your neighborhood. Hang up the signs around the school site and have students practice reading them.

PAGE 260

ACTIVITY: See *"Teaching the Picture Pages."*

Supplementary Work Sheets

Practice printing.

a a _____

b b _____

c c _____

d d _____

e e _____

f f _____

g g _____

h h _____

i i _____

j j _____

k k _____

l l _____

m m _____

n n _____

o o _____

p p _____

q q _____

r r _____

s s _____

t t _____

u u _____

v v _____

w w _____

x x _____

y y _____

z z _____

Practice printing.

A A _____
B B _____
C C _____
D D _____
E E _____
F F _____
G G _____
H H _____
I I _____
J J _____
K K _____
L L _____
M M _____
N N _____
O O _____
P P _____
Q Q _____
R R _____
S S _____
T T _____
U U _____
V V _____
W W _____
X X _____
Y Y _____
Z Z _____

Match

a	F	h	J	o	R
b	C	i	K	p	T
c	E	j	M	q	Q
d	A	k	H	r	S
e	B	l	L	s	U
f	G	m	I	t	P
g	D	n	N	u	O
v	X	Q	y	J	b
w	V	R	a	L	n
x	Z	Y	d	B	f
y	W	U	g	N	l
z	Y	A	u	M	h
		D	q	F	j
		G	r	H	m

Match

1. I am   He's

2. You are   They're

3. He is   It's

4. She is   I'm

5. It is   You're

6. We are   She's

7. They are   We're

Write the contraction for the words.

1. I am _____

2. You are_____

3. He is _____

4. She is _____

5. It is _____

6. We are _____

7. They are _____

Write the words for the contractions.

1. I'm _____   5. It's _____

2. You're _____   6. We're_____

3. He's _____   7. They're_____

4. She's _____

Use this page after page 6 from the text, _Survival English_, Book 1.

Miguel Garcia is from Mexico. He is from Tijuana, Mexico. Now he is living in the United States. He is living in San Diego, California. His address is 8674 44th Street. His telephone number is 555 – 9532.

1. What's his name? _____

2. What country is he from? _____

3. What city is he from? _____

4. What's his address now? _____

    _____

5. What's his telephone number? _____

6. What's your name? _____

7. What country are you from? _____

8. What's your address now? _____

    _____

Use this page after page 26 from the text, *Survival English*, Book 1.

Practice your writing.

1. How are you?

   _____

2. I'm sick.

   _____

3. What's the matter?

   _____

4. My stomach hurts.

   _____

5. I hope you feel better.

   _____

6. My chest hurts.

   _____

7. My neck hurts.

   _____

8. My shoulder hurts.

   _____

Use this page after page 91 from the text, _Survival English_, Book 1.

1. I'm not coming to school tomorrow.

   _____ going to the dentist.

2. He isn't coming to school tomorrow.

   _____ going to the doctor.

3. She isn't coming to school tomorrow.

   _____ going to the work.

4. They aren't coming to school tomorrow.

   _____ going to the doctor.

5. Ann _____ coming to school tomorrow.

   _____ going to the dentist.

6. Bob _____ coming to school tomorrow

   _____ going to the dentist.

7. Ann and Bob_____ coming to school.

   _____ going to the dentist.

8. Fran _____ coming to school tomorrow.

   _____ going to the doctor.

9. Paul _____ coming to school tomorrow.

   _____ going to work.

Use this page after page 106 from the text, _Survival English_, Book 1.

Yes, it does.	No, it doesn't.
Yes, they do.	No, they don't.

1. Does your tooth hurt? _____

2. Do your ears hurt? _____

3. Does your stomach hurt? _____

4. Does your arm hurt? _____

5. Do your shoulders hurt? _____

6. Does your back hurt? _____

7. Do your feet hurt? _____

8. Does your head hurt? _____

9. Do your eyes hurt? _____

10. Does your back hurt? _____

11. Do your knees hurt? _____

12. Do your leg hurt? _____

Use this page after page 106 from the text, _Survival English,_ Book 1.

Practice your writing.

1. I drive to school.

   _____

2. How do you go to school?

   _____

3. I take the bus.

   _____

4. She walks to school.

   _____

5. I drive to work.

   _____

6. He takes the bus to school.

   _____

7. She walks to work.

   _____

8. He rides a bicycle to school.

   _____

Use this page after page 117 from the text, _Survival English_, Book 1.